FIRMLY PLANTED PUBLICATIONS
An imprint of Equipped for Life Ministries, Dallas, Texas

I0112119

Acceptable to God without being Saved?

Saul was! Could others be today?

B. Dale Taliaferro

Acceptable to God without being Saved?
Published by Firmly Planted Publications
An imprint of Equipped for Life Ministries

Copyright © 2015 by B. Dale Taliaferro
International Standard Book Number:
978-1-950072-07-1

For information:
Equipped for Life Ministries
P.O. Box 12013
Dallas, Texas 75225
U.S.A.

Library of Congress Control Number:

Revised Edition 2019

Acknowledgement

I always have so many to thank for making each book a reality. I am so blessed to have so many who express their love towards me and my family in this way. Thanks to Carol Trebes, Curtis Tucker, and Maritza Ortiz for proof reading multiple versions of this book. And a special thanks goes to Maritza who also formatted the book for me. Without her patience in handling my tedious edits the book would never have been finished. And without my wife, Waunee, who had to deal with the copy rite issues, the book cover, the printer, the ISBN obtainment, and all communications to the printer, I fear the book would never had made it into print. Thank you all for your tireless and sacrificial work. May our Lord use it for His glory in drawing all men to Himself.

Table of Contents

Preface to the Revised Edition

This series of books was written during my spiritual journey. As a result, I now find the need to go back through each volume and make some necessary corrections and updates. I really didn't understand how many preconceived ideas that I was working from and that were still hindering my comprehension of the real message of the Bible. I still needed to confront several issues and hold them under the microscope of God's Word. For the sake of simplicity, I will summarize those issues here:

1. I developed a better understanding of the historical situations of some very important passages which changed my thinking relative to their meaning. As a result, the unpardonable sin has been revised. Basically, the unpardonable sin is a rejection of Jesus as the Messiah by the first century Jewish people, resulting in a delay of their earthly kingdom, promised to them by God in the OT, and to their missing entering into that kingdom in their mortal bodies.

2. I finally was able to move past my theological prejudices concerning Acts 16:31 and Eph. 2:8-9 by understanding salvation and faith Biblically. As a result, I have found that the Bible does not describe a person as being saved from hell because salvation never refers to a deliverance from hell once-for-all or in any other way. Consequently, these two classic passages on salvation have nothing to do with a rescue from hell with a promise of heaven. Those ideas have been read into these passages without any substantiation.

3. Since no one was ever described as a "saved person" by *initially* trusting in Jesus, I am led to reframe from do-

ing that as well. I eventually realized that even the apostles were not described as "saved persons" after they had initially trusted in Jesus. *Salvation is not a standing or status before God that guarantees a person a heavenly home and an escape from hell.* Nor is it a permanent, unchangeable condition that is reached by initially (or continually) trusting in Jesus. We can be saved from temptations and sins, but we can't be saved from hell and given heaven due to a simple trust in Jesus.

4. Finally, I realized that while there is no concept in the NT that can be likened to the traditional idea of a "saved person" in Christian teachings, there is a NT concept of a *salvation that is taking place presently*. As a result, it is biblical to describe people as being saved from temptations and sins but not as having been saved once for all from hell with a guarantee of heaven. Since the Bible doesn't do that, neither should we. It is easy to see how this reinforces the new understanding of Acts 16:30-31 and Eph. 2:8-9.

With these discoveries, I was able to reach a consistent concept of salvation with nothing but the Bible as my guide. The biggest correction that I have needed in these volumes is to distinguish between a *spiritual* salvation that is defined as an ongoing deliverance from temptations and sins from the traditional, but mistaken, idea of a *spiritual* salvation that supposedly takes place at the moment of initial faith in Jesus and that supposedly obtains a deliverance from hell. While the former is clearly Biblical; the latter is a creation by men alone.

Preface

This book will build upon my last one, *The Prodigal Paradigm, The Bible's Real Storyline.* As a result, I won't try to defend the principles I set forth in that book; I will take them for granted here. This book demonstrates how Saul illustrates all the conclusions arrived at in that prequel. There is a vast difference between justification and salvation in the Scriptures, and we minimize that distinction to our own confusion and detriment. And to make matters worse, neither term is used in Christian theological circles the way they are in the Bible.

The truth is justification and salvation can be clearly distinguished and can be easily shown to occur at different times. But if the Bible is made to conform to man's fallible systematization of it, which we know by the term Systematic Theology, these false assumptions will never be brought under the scrutiny that is required to test their validity.

Just as God meant for Judas to be the face for divine grace, He meant the apostle Paul to be the face for the distinction between a person who is *acceptable to God* and a person who is *saved by Jesus.* In Saul's life we clearly have presented to us these two separate issues. Only an unwillingness to take the Bible as it stands will produce a resistance to these divine distinctions.

The repercussions of these distinctions will not find a ready acceptance with some leaders within Christianity. We must not be naïve to think that everyone will be like John the Baptist who was willing to have his own significance decrease in the eyes of the world in order for Jesus' significance to increase.

The questions are, "Will we be humble enough to accept the Biblical distinctions? Or will we respond like many of the Scribes and Pharisees did in the first century when Jesus offered Himself as their promised Messiah?"

I actually did not want to walk down this path myself because, having been in the ministry for over forty-nine years, I know how critical and judgmental Christians can be. I think they all learned it from me! But God used the same method on me to open my eyes that He used on Saul: *He goaded me until I became open to other possibilities!* That is one of the reasons I am so confident about the principles outlined in this book. And believe me, I know how *that* sounds!

> If the distinction is maintained between a person's approval by God and his salvation by Jesus, no longer will Western Christianity have a corner on the market of truth.

Once I became open to the possibility that such a distinction might exist, and I began to apply it in my own study of the Scriptures, I quickly realized what a difference this made in the message set forth in the Bible. Some passages that I couldn't make sense out of became instantly clear. Other passages took on very different interpretations. After I set aside the theology that I had been taught and took the message of the Bible as it actually stands, I realized its focus shifted from a "heaven and hell" paradigm to a "Father-son" paradigm. This latter paradigm centers attention on an unbelievably loving and gracious God who is seeking His lost, wandering children, who repeatedly stray away from Him just as one would naturally expect dumb sheep to do. The Father-son paradigm is built upon a relationship of love because of which the Father seeks fellowship with His estranged sons and daughters.

While I realize that the message in this book, as in its prequel, will be a difficult perspective to receive for some, it is my hope that it will at least drive us back to the Scriptures to test what we've been taught and to examine what is being said here. But if it only drives us back to our accepted theological resources, we will remain in the dark of night, rehashing the same old issues that have long ago exposed the weaknesses in our theological perspectives.

It is my prayer that you discover in the exposition presented here the amazing grace and the long-suffering love of the God of the Bible and fall more deeply in love with Him than ever before. He is ever-waiting on you to enrich your relationship with Him if you already have a vital one. His blessings are sure to salve all the hurts and wounds that you have incurred in life whether or not you've been "in the far country."[1] He is ready to forgive and lavish upon you blessings that meet your deepest longings. By His creation of you, He has set a sense of eternity within your heart[2] and that mystery can only be satisfied through a relationship with Him. He is waiting. Will you come?

And how exactly do you come? You come by faith alone. And what do you need to believe? Believe that in Jesus are all the treasures of knowledge and wisdom[3] that unlock all the questions you have and provides all the solutions that you will ever need. Believe that He died on the cross to take care of every sin that you've ever committed and that has separated you from

---

[1] Cf., Lk. 15:13.
[2] Eccl. 3:11.
[3] Col. 2:1-3.

the God that loves you so profoundly and longs to establish an intimate walk with you daily. Nothing that you've ever done is so terrible that God won't forgive it. He knew the gravity of every sin we'd all commit, and so He sent Jesus to remove them all so that we could experience life as God always meant it to be lived.

By your creation, He made you for Himself. He created you in His image so that a full, satisfying, and purposeful relationship between the two of you could exist. As a consequence of this privilege, He has commissioned each of us to walk in such a way that we will represent Him well in all that we do. The apostle Paul would summarize these concepts in his pithy statement to the Corinthians, which even deals with amoral activities, saying,

> "Whether, then, you eat or drink or whatever you do, do all for the glory of God." (1Cor. 10:31)

That is the message of the Bible, and, for the most part, we are all agreed on it. The point at which we differ is how Jesus relates to this. While that is no small issue, the life of Saul was given to put all of these matters into their proper place.

My journey began as I looked more closely at verses that I knew didn't fit easily into the system that I had been taught. Now I praise God for my previously troubled heart because it has led me into a new perspective that makes me stand in such awe of God that I can't help myself in wanting to share it with others. May you know from experience what I'm talking about!

Introduction

I had the privilege of conducting the funeral of Sam Stone a number of years ago. Sam was a Jewish immigrant to the United States and, until he met his future bride and wife of 50 plus years, centered his life around his Jewish family and friends. But once he met the love of his life, his perspective began to change a bit. For the rest of his life, the one constant in Sam's life was the love he had for Dixie. It radiated in every look he made in her direction. Sometime in the early days of their relationship Dixie led Sam to faith in Jesus Christ. And they grew ever closer with one another as they grew in their faith.

Dixie asked me to perform the funeral services for Sam, mainly because I had been their Sunday school class teacher for almost ten years and had gotten to know them fairly well. When I rose to give his eulogy at the funeral, I noticed that all of his Jewish friends were sitting in the pews on my left and his Christian friends were sitting in the pews on my right. I had asked the Lord in the days leading up to the service for a way to engage all those who would be present. My goal was to have all of them think about God's commission to each one present to live a vibrant, spiritual life for the Lord God of Israel, representing Him in all that he did. He answered my prayers with a clarity on the Jewish-Christian situation that I have never forgotten.

This revelation wasn't even part of *God's goading* me for I received it so willingly and without hesitation because it fit perfectly into what I had always been taught about Christianity's dependence upon the OT Jewish faith. Jesus, after all, was first and foremost Israel's Messiah, and He must be received even today as such if we are to believe the apostle John's purpose statement in his Gospel. There he explained that his whole book was written...

> "... that you (the reader) may believe that Jesus is the Christ (Greek equivalent to Messiah), the Son of God (an appositive further describing the Messiah) ..." (John 20:31, parentheses mine)

Unfortunately, believing in Jesus as the Jewish Messiah is not a truth that is emphasized today for no other reason than it doesn't fit our current theological commitments very well.

I began my eulogy by reminding all present how much Sam loved and cared for them all, how Dixie had led Sam to trust in Jesus, and how I agreed with Sam's religious beliefs. They were probably thinking at that point that I was referring only to Sam's Christian beliefs. But I clarified that with my next comment which seemed to jolt the left side of the chapel a bit. I said,

> "Like Sam, I believe that the Jewish faith, as that faith is revealed in the Jewish Holy Scriptures, is absolutely, one hundred percent true . . . and for that reason I am, as Sam was, a Christian."

The furrowed brows were evident all the way to the back pew. It was obvious to me that those present on the left side of the chapel had never heard a statement like that before.

So I continued by explaining that Christianity was not a different religion; it was, in fact, the partial completion of the Jewish faith. *And as such, no Jewish person is leaving his faith when he trusts in Jesus.* Rather, he or she has simply become convinced that Jesus fulfilled enough of the OT prophecies about the Messiah to prove that He was indeed that person.

Now these comments are not new or original. You have probably heard them before as I had. But the point is that if it is true that *Christianity is a continuation and partial fulfillment of the Jewish faith*, then we ought to expect closer connections between Judaism and Christianity when it comes to almost all the doctrines of Scripture. While many, if not most, Christians would readily agree with that premise, yet it is quite astounding how few have carefully considered the ramifications of it.

> The Christian faith does not replace the Jewish faith; it is a continuation of it.

I am not denying that there can be new revelation because it is self-evidently true that there has been. But there should be a *consistency* between how a person found approval with God in the OT and how a person finds approval with God in the NT. There ought to be a *consistency* in how a person was justified in the OT with how a person is justified in the NT. And in the same way, there ought to be a parallel, at least in some fashion, between the concept of salvation in the OT and the presentation of salvation in the NT. While God can and did give new revelation concerning the idea of salvation, none of it nullified the concepts of salvation set forth in the OT. There really is a *continuity* between the Testaments, and it is the goal of the first two books in this series to clarify and display that fact.

Saul, who eventually becomes the apostle Paul, personifies for us the divinely intended, spiritual continuity between the OT people of God and the NT people of God. In so doing, he aids us in understanding the Biblical concepts of faith in God, forgiveness, justification, sanctification, and God's demand of righteousness. But he gives us a very different picture of these

Biblical doctrines from the one many theologians espouse. At least that is true in my own experience.

He also helps us to be more greatly amazed at the new revelation that he found in Jesus. He was a zealous, committed follower of the God of Israel and one who was eagerly waiting for his God's Messiah to appear. But initially he was blinded to the possibility that Jesus could be that Messiah. He did not tell us exactly why that was the case. It could have been the fact that Jesus did not fulfill all the prophecies that were predicted of Him. Or it could have been that he was trusting the conclusions of his peers who had had more exposure to Jesus than he did. Either way, he was led to the wrong conclusion about Jesus initially.

His zeal for his faith, a belief system that he had learned from the most gifted Bible teachers of his day, kept him from the new revelations about that faith that he cherished so much. Saul was struggling with the facts before his face. *Once he received them, he became the face of a spiritual transition. Saul shows us how a person moved from a belief in God and a walk with Him before the time of Jesus to a walk with God after receiving divine resources from Jesus for a new kind of walk.*

And that transition is still going on today! It is possible to have a trust in and a walk with God apart from believing in Jesus. In fact, a person can believe in God and pursue a faithful, obedient walk with God even though he has rejected Jesus. Saul clearly illustrates these truths for us. If we are able to receive them, our *evangelism* should become more potent than ever.

Section One

The Path that Led Saul to Jesus

Chapter 1
Stephen's Distinctives

The historical context that introduces Saul to us is the ministry, arrest, mock trial, and execution by stoning of Stephen, a disciple of the Lord and one of the first deacons of the early church. It seems readily apparent that Saul's experience with Stephen is one of God's most explicit *goads*,[1] intended to lead Saul to faith in Jesus. As Stephen was performing great wonders and signs among the people, he told his audiences about Jesus and the claims He had made of being the promised Messiah. He explained how Jesus proved His claims by the miracles He performed and by His many fulfillments of the Jewish Scriptures.

So, in a very similar way to Jesus' ministry, the signs and wonders that Stephen performed demonstrated that the God of Israel was involved in his ministry while the OT Scriptures proved that what he was preaching was what the prophets had indicated must take place.[2] If one was to compare Stephen to Jesus in terms of his ministry, his character, and even his actions at his death, he would find a great many similarities. Stephen had become conformed to the image of his Lord,[3] becoming a model[4] for all who would follow him in history, even for Saul, an accomplice in his killing. While Saul thought he was being obedient to the Scriptures in seeking Stephen's death,[5] God revealed

---

[1] Acts 26:14.

[2] Acts 26:22-23.

[3] Rom. 8:28-29a.

[4] Cf., 1Cor. 11:1.

[5] Cf., e.g., Ex. 20:3-7; John 16:1-2.

to him later that he had been terribly wrong.[1]

As Stephen continued to minister in the name of Jesus, eventually some men began to appear to argue with Stephen over whether Jesus was really the promised Messiah. They couldn't gainsay the miracles that Stephen was performing. They were wonderful signs confirming God's involvement in his ministry and in his message.[2] How does a person deny that a lame man was healed when he is seen walking, leaping, and praising God?[3] How does one deny that all the various infirmities caused by demonic activity have been healed when the demons have been cast out and the infirmities are no longer present?[4]

As the debate continued, it became obvious that those opposing Stephen were badly losing ground. As one might expect from a close defensive-minded, and aggressive people, they bribed some men to falsely testify against Stephen to negate his defense of Jesus.[5] With the help of these false witnesses, Stephen's opponents stirred up the people, the elders, and the scribes, finally gaining the upper hand.[6] At that point they dragged Stephen before the high council of the Jews.

*Their actions show us how susceptible **followers of God** are to the sin that indwells them.* My previous book, *The Prodigal Paradigm,* has argued that all the Jewish people that Jesus, His apostles, and their disciples after them dealt with in the Gospels and in the Book of Acts were followers of the God of Israel. In our contemporary, but unbiblical parlance, we would call them *believers,*

---

[1] Acts 9:4-6; Gal. 1:13-24; 1Tim. 1:13-16.

[2] Cf., Mk. 2:10-12; Matt. 10:5-8; John 3:2; Heb. 2:3-4.

[3] Cf., Acts 3:8; 6:8; 8:6-7.

[4] Cf., Acts 4:29-30; 5:12, 14-16.

[5] Acts 6:10.

[6] Acts 6:11-12.

a term that needs to be reevaluated and redefined in light of the Scriptures.

When Stephen was brought to the chambers of the Sanhedrin, it seems more than likely that Saul was already present for Stephen's hearing. As he would confess later in reference to others who were condemned to die, he "cast his pebble" against anyone who believed in Jesus as the promised Jewish Messiah. "Casting a pebble," apparently, was the means of voting on the guilt or innocence of a person brought before the high council.[1] Saul accepted and followed the reasoning of the educated, like-minded religious leaders to whom he felt accountable. *His convictions reflected the consensus of his peers who were devoted to God and were very reputable.* But his bond with them, tied together by their rejection of Jesus, would break eventually. Each one of us will be brought to the same cross-roads. Will we imitate Saul or remain in the comfort provided by a commonly held consensus? There is no pressure like religious peer pressure.

Since the witnesses and at least a few of the leaders moved straight from the chambers of the high council to the place where they stoned Stephen, Saul would probably not have been involved unless he had a chance to interact with the person and his arguments. Saul was an intellectual, not a raving fanatic.

Certainly he was enraged at the Messianic Jews of his day, but his rage came from reason and loyalty, not from emotions alone. But whether he had been in the council chambers or had joined the procession leading Stephen outside the city for stoning, in the end, it is an absolute certainty that Saul had agreed with the verdict and supported the stoning of Stephen.[2] Against

---

[1] Cf., Acts 26:10.

[2] Acts 8:1. Cf., Acts 26:10-11.

15

this divine goad, he kicked, resisting God's leading and turning away His grace. In Stephen's dying testimony, he *explicitly* accused all of his executioners of doing this same thing and in so doing of repeating the sins of their forefathers when they killed the prophets God had sent to them.

What kind of man was Saul agreeing to execute? It was here, deep within his soul, that Saul felt the greatest force of God's goading. We all ought to praise God that He is able to convict even the most zealous and convinced man among us.

But, speaking from personal experience, I can tell you that there are few hurdles in life that are as difficult to surmount as the relinquishment of previously held convictions formed from the hard work of study and research pursued through many years of post-graduate education. This is especially true if your teachers were considered to be some of the best in the world.

Saul was about to be put into a crucible, and his understanding of the faith God had revealed in the Scriptures was about to receive its most severe testing. The dross would become evident to him, and he would have to continue his spiritual journey in opposition to those he continued to hold in such high esteem. God may call some of us to do the same thing.

A Man of Good Reputation

When the early church was looking for men to take over the task of feeding those in need, the apostles didn't look for men who had money to give, or for men who were administratively organized, or for men who had conflict-resolution skills. That might be what the church would do today after hiring expert consultants to help solve such internal problems within the church. But the apostles looked for men of good reputation.

The Greek term translated here *good reputation* comes from the root μαρτυρ. The group of words flowing from that root all have to do with giving a witness, giving a testimony, or giving evidence of something known or believed to be true. We get the English word *martyr* from that same root because the term eventually developed in meaning. It came to describe a person giving his life for what he believed to be true. He might witness for Christ even though it meant dying a martyr's death.

So, Stephen and the other six men chosen to serve tables[1] were called deacons[2] because of the service they would render. But these were all men who had lived their faith attractively before the world around them. Since their walk matched their talk, their beliefs were held in high esteem because their character and lifestyles were recognized as results of their faith.

It must have been a difficult pill to swallow for Saul to condemn a man so well respected. It must have eaten away at his soul, knowing that a man of such standing was killed because of doctrinal differences so slight and so tentative that the same person could actually argue for both sides of the debate. For someone intent on pleasing God, there is no guilt like being responsible for the condemnation of a good man. But the voice of guilt can be silenced, and usually is, in direct proportion to the confidence arising within him that he is serving God even when in reality he isn't.[3]

---

[1] Acts 6:2.

[2] The infinitive *to serve* in Acts 6:2 is διακονειν, and the noun διακονος is used by Paul to describe the qualifications for the office of *deacon* within the church in 1Tim. 3:8-13.

[3] Cf., John 16:1-2.

Full of the Spirit and Wisdom

In addition to having a good reputation because of their character and lifestyle, the men chosen to serve the early church also manifested both the Holy Spirit and the wisdom of God. Luke described these men as those "full of the Spirit." This is a completely unintelligible statement for many "believers" (i.e., followers of Jesus Christ) today simply because they have had little to no accurate teaching on the ministry of the Spirit of God in their lives.

The fullness or filling of the Spirit is a dynamic ministry within the soul of the so-called believer. The Spirit of God provides this ministry to everyone who *consciously trusts Him* to provide it, enabling that trusting person to carry out what he knows God wants him to do. What he may have found impossible to do on his own becomes a natural success story if the Spirit is trusted to provide what is specifically needed to accomplish what God is leading him to do.

It is by no coincidence that the Spirit of God moved the physician Luke to describe Stephen as a man full of the Spirit "and of wisdom." The Spirit of God was not given to by-pass the mind or the study of the Word of God. He was not given to work independently in the life of a person any more than Jesus came to work independently from the Father who had sent Him. Just as Jesus came to do the will of the Father who sent Him, the Holy Spirit was given to empower the trusting person to do the Father's will now made known through Jesus.[1]

Stephen, who had been sitting at the feet of the apostles as they were studying and expounding "the Word of God,"[2] gained

---

[1] Cf., Heb. 1:1-2.

[2] Acts 2:42; 6:2, 4, 7.

the understanding he needed as he learned "all the things that Jesus had taught"[1] the original apostles. This truth, then, became the foundation for the Spirit's leading. And as always, the Spirit's leading is the wise application to real situations of the knowledge gained from God's written word. But the Spirit does not just lead the trusting person as we will see in the following description of Stephen.

Full of Faith and the Holy Spirit

Just two verses later Luke employed the phrase "full of faith and of the Holy Spirit" in place of the phrase used earlier, "full of the Spirit and of wisdom." While the former phrase joined two complementary concepts, the Spirit and wisdom, to portray a walk that yields a good reputation, now the focus turned to the two responsibilities of the two different agents involved in such a walk. Man is responsible to believe. And the Holy Spirit is responsible to produce the supernatural, spiritual life needed to live successfully for God in a fallen world. The Word of God sets before each Christian the content that he is responsible to believe. As he relies upon the Spirit for power, virtue, and wisdom, he steps forward to implement what the Spirit has led him to do from God's Word.

The Bible instructs, and the Holy Spirit enables. Both are needed for spiritual victory over the temptations that we encounter and the trials that we must face. But these two work in tandem with, never in isolation from, one another.

---

[1] Matt. 28:19; Acts 1:8.

His Angelic Countenance

I was privileged to know a man named John Saville. John had an amazing walk with God. He loved to be in the back at meetings, supporting what was going on without ever being in the forefront so the eyes of those attending and receiving the benefit from the meeting never fell upon him. It wasn't that John was hesitant to take a stand for Christ; he looked for opportunities to share his faith. It wasn't that John thought his personal beliefs were somehow irrelevant to others; he didn't. John's face was extremely disfigured due to the number of skin cancer operations he had experienced and the laser, radiation, and chemo therapies he had undergone. And he was very conscious of making others feel uncomfortable in his presence. But John's heart was as pure and as smooth as his face now is in the presence of Jesus Christ for all eternity.

I was privileged to be in John's hospital room the day before he died. As always we talked about Jesus. Nothing else really mattered to either of us. And I can tell you that I can hardly write this without crying. Well, let me rephrase that: I can tell you that I'm *not* writing this now without crying. Of all the men that have been involved in my personal ministry, none possessed the spirituality that John did. He would often offer only a simple comment that would change my perspective completely. His trust in Jesus was as reassuring as it was calming.

Well, on that last night before he died, John and I talked about walking with Jesus. For my own benefit and because I often get some opposition to the message I teach on the Christian life by those who do not seem to understand how to live in dependence upon the Holy Spirit as the Scriptures teach, I asked John a simple question: "John, how does a person *know for sure* that he is filled with the Spirit?" John's marred face belied the spiritual purity, wisdom, and great compassion that he constantly demonstrated toward everyone with whom he spoke. He replied, "Dale, it really is very simple. A person is filled with the Spirit when there is no more *self* involved."

At his statement, I burst into tears not only because his truthful answer pierced my heart, but also because he was the perfect reflection of the truth he was communicating to me. *Selflessness is not natural, not even for a Christian.* It is the spiritual fruit that comes from a reliance on the Holy Spirit for everything needed to follow Jesus.[1]

The Christian life is not about what the Christian is able to do; it is about what Jesus is able to do *through* that Christian as he yields himself to the leading and power of the Spirit of God. We, John liked to say, never get better. It is the Spirit within us that must produce all that Jesus or all that His heavenly Father is requiring from us. While John's face may not have looked like the face of an angel at that moment, his heart and his words would surely have matched any one of God's heavenly hosts.

Stephen, in the same way, not only demonstrated the power, grace, wisdom, and miraculous powers of God, his face also shone like the face of an angel. Whether we take the phrase as a reflection of an angel or of the risen Lord Jesus, it is a certainty that God's will is to transform each of us into the image of Jesus so that we may live *a mirrored life*. The source of that life is Jesus. We only reflect to others what is shining upon us, much like the moon doesn't produce any light of its own but only reflects the light of the sun. The brightness and persistence of that light

---

[1] E.g., cf., Gal. 5:22-23. See especially that aspect of the Spirit's fruit called "self-control."

measures the degree of our conformity[1] to the image of Christ.[2]

To condemn a man of such spirituality must have weighed heavily upon Saul. He had to have been a truly torn man. Half of him felt quite satisfied about his fervent defense of his faith. The other half was questioning why a truly wonderful man was being put to death. God was goading and the strikes were being felt deep within Saul's soul, troubling a conscience that only wanted to please God in all that he did.

Have you experienced this phenomenon without realizing what it was all about? God troubles our conscience so that we would ask questions about the circumstances that face us. He desires that we not simply seek another equilibrium that we can live in; rather, He wants us to pursue truths that can set us free and enable us to live an entirely different life altogether. To merely salve the conscience so we can continue to live independently of God is to silence the voice of God within calling us home. A day comes when that voice can no longer be heard, and we are left alone. The independence that we had so zealously sought will become a very frightening place to be when we finally realize that our sense of self-sufficiency was really a mirage and not the oasis we thought it was.

Saul was a man who walked with God. The Scriptures tell us that he was a righteous man who was all that God wanted him to be. Yet, he was not a Stephen! There was something about Stephen's life that he couldn't grasp;[3] it was something that was evident and yet unrealistic at the same time.[4] And this was more

---

[1] Rom. 8:28-29.

[2] 2Cor. 3:18.

[3] Cf., 1Cor. 2:14-15.

[4] 2Cor. 4:7-11.

than zeal because Saul had that.[1] It was more than tenacity for he had that too.[2] It was more than intelligence because Saul was known for his sharp mind.[3]

What Saul experienced as he watched Stephen interact with all of his accusers was a Power that gave him the ability to be gracious yet steadfastly truthful, to be humble and yet strong, and to be convincing yet forgiving at the same time. What Saul witnessed in Stephen was a life that he had never encountered before. It was so noteworthy to Saul that he would later write these words:

> "And I was with you in weakness and in fear and in much trembling. And my message and my preaching were not in persuasive words of wisdom, but in a demonstration of the Spirit and of power, that your faith should not rest on the wisdom of men, but on the power of God." (1Cor. 2:3-5)

What was so attractive to Saul was the power that the Spirit of God enabled Stephen to manifest. While his words were persuasive, the power in which he spoke them was beyond comprehension and added to them an unassailable character. Saul could not answer Stephen's points,[4] but his religious training kept him from being convinced. That still needed to be overcome in Saul as it does in each of us today.

---

[1] Gal. 1:14.

[2] Gal. 1:13.

[3] Acts 26:24-29.

[4] Acts 6:10; 7:51-53, 54-55.

Chapter 2
Stephen's Defense

Stephen's defense is quite illuminating on several fronts. It gives us an inspired summary of Israel's history and an equally infallible account of the nation's spiritual heritage and status before God. If the former issue is not deemed important, the latter issue ought to pique our interest. It is one of the goals of this book to demonstrate by the life of Saul that the people of Israel, chosen by God to serve Him uniquely, both in the OT as well as in the Gospels, were following the God that they believed had set them apart for Himself. At the time of Jesus they were *not* a nation that denied their own accountability to the one, true God. They knew that God existed and that He was a rewarder of those who sought Him. And they understood that He had chosen them above all other nations to serve Him in a unique way.

If it can be shown that the people of Israel already maintained a spiritual relationship with God, then none of the Gospels can be said to be evangelistic in the modern sense of that term. And indeed, Israel did have such a relationship with God as Stephen's defense clearly established.

> Notwithstanding his personal zeal, Saul was typical of the average Jew in his day.

Saul described himself as belonging to the tribe of Benjamin. He was, by his own admission, a "Hebrew of the Hebrews," and thus the perfect representative of the belief system of the whole nation. He may have been more formally trained in this faith and more zealous in his practice of it, but his was the same faith that each Jew possessed essentially.

And this is no stretch to believe that the rest of the nation possessed the same faith that Saul did. After all, the people were being led by such godly men as Nicodemus and all those who were in agreement with him when he went to Jesus by night. Just as Nicodemus and Joseph of Arimathea ministered to the Sanhedrin, Zachariah the priest and his wife, walking blamelessly before the Lord, ministered to the tribe of Levi and the priests that served with them. And we must not forget the common people such as Joseph and Mary who were both righteous and honored by God. The spirituality of Simeon and Anna must not be missed since both were chosen to announce the Messiah's birth and to identify Him in His infancy. When you come to think of it, there is not the slightest doubt about the spiritual walk of anyone mentioned in the NT until the time Jesus began His ministry and became the dividing issue among the people, even of those of the same household and faith.[1]

If opposition to truth is supposed to be an infallible guide to a spurious faith that lacks any connection to God, then let us begin casting stones at all, not some, but all, of the denominations that currently represent different views of what is *assumed* to be the true teaching of the Bible. In most cases, the various congregations of a particular denomination can't even agree among themselves about every issue on which they must take a position. So the Presbyterian churches have the PCUSA's and the PCA's and the EPC's. The Baptists? Well, last time I counted, there were over thirty-two different kinds of Baptists!

---

[1] Cf., Matt. 10:34-39.

But few would be so bold as to suggest that all the other Christians in all the other denominations are people possessing a spurious faith and lacking any connection to the God that they worship every Sunday. If anyone should be so bold, he needs to realize that he must point his finger at his own denomination as well.

The same thing was happening in the first century. Some followers of God thought Jesus was a God-send; they thought He was their promised Messiah. Others questioned this conclusion for various reasons. Should we understand this difference of opinion to be any different from what we see in all the denominations around us? I don't think so. The people of Israel could disagree on all kinds of issues, just like our denominations do today, without evidencing any *supposed* eternal condemnation.

In Stephen's defense, he will confirm the perspective that I have taken here. He will demonstrate for us that Israel has always been a special people who have followed God from their inception as a nation, and even before that moment, to the time of Jesus' earthly ministry. So listen carefully to the arguments given to his accusers and realize that Saul stood firmly in the middle of the tradition that Stephen was describing. Believing in Jesus did not put anyone there; believing in Jesus put him further down the same road that the OT traditions paved for the NT believers. As Jesus repeatedly said in the gospel of John, He role was to connect His followers with the God of the OT.

The God of Glory Appeared to Abraham

We really don't know the specific means that God used to make Himself known to Abraham, but the text is clear that He appeared to him in some fashion. It seems most probable that

His appearance[1] was like the one He sustained with Adam and Eve as He walked with them physically in the Garden of Eden. Adam and Eve could see, hear, touch, and talk with this person ~ even have fellowship with Him over a meal. Abraham seems to have had those same experiences.[2]

In addition, this appearance was probably one of many throughout Abraham's walk of faith. The OT history that Moses gave us states that God appeared to Abraham more than once.[3] And we are correct to expect that an intimate relationship was developed through these various encounters. After all, Abraham became known as the "friend of God,"[4] and such a description presumes a close relationship with God.[5]

Abraham had been walking with God for a very long time, probably for most of his adult life. It is possible, and I believe very likely, that Abraham had been walking with God for twenty-five to fifty years *before* he came to the event in his life that Moses used to describe his justification. Consequently, Moses was not signifying that the instance that he chose to describe was Abraham's initial faith nor was it the only time that Abraham was justified. Rather, Moses was, by describing this particular event, explaining the process by which Abraham became known as the "friend of God." He lived in communion with God and whenever God revealed new information to him, he believed God and was guided by the new revelation.

To take this episode in the life of Abraham as Abraham's initial faith is to miss the point that Stephen, and Moses before him,

---

[1] Acts 7:2.

[2] Cf., e.g., Gen. 18:3-8.

[3] Cf., Acts 7:2; Gen. 12:7; 17:1; 18:1; etc.

[4] Js. 2:23; Isa. 41:8; 2Chron. 20:7.

[5] Cf., John 15:13-15.

were trying to make. Justification is God's declaration that a particular response is righteous. In other words, justification is God's disclosure of the kind of response that He finds acceptable. Every faith response is a righteous response, and every righteous response finds approval with God.

In justification God justifies what He sees in man. As I explained in the prequel to this book, we have terribly misunderstood the concept of justification, among other major issues, because we have forced it to denote a legal paradigm denoting guilt or pardon, and condemnation or forgiveness. Like Cinderella's slipper, that is a shoe that doesn't fit the Biblical usages of the term.

Israel Entered the Land, Serving God

Stephen then reminded his judges that the Israelites, who are, Biblically speaking, the descendants of Jacob, believed and followed God *all their lives*, including *before* they went down to Egypt, *during* their time in Egypt, and *after* their exodus from Egypt. When they finally entered the Promised Land after their wilderness wanderings for forty years, they *served and worshipped the God* who had brought them out of Egypt with a strong, outstretched hand and miraculous signs. But none had a perfect walk; most were stubborn, even rebellious. Just like us.

Stephen's testimony established the fact that the second generation of Israelites, continued in the same relationship with God that their parents had experienced over the previous forty years. But because of their parents' sin of unbelief at Kadesh Barnea, God judged them in the wilderness, refusing to permit them to enter the Promised Land. The second generation believed in and walked with God[1] even though that walk can only

---

[1] Cf., Gen. 17:8. God promised to be the God of those who entered the Promised Land.

be described as inconsistent and at times either half-hearted or fully rebellious. The taint and corruption in their walk demonstrate the influence of indwelling sin in their lives. They struggled with it just as every Christian does today.[1]

> Jesus' audiences in the four Gospels were of this same faith and struggled to walk approvingly before the one, true God they believed in.

But it is on point to observe that at no time in Israel's history is anyone ever sent to any part of the nation to evangelize its people. There was never a need in the whole course of Israel's history for such action to be taken.

Consequently, when the NT began there was no indication that the nation's relationship with God had changed in the slightest. The Gospel writers call the people of Israel God's people[2] to whom Jesus was sent to create a revival[3] that would impact the way they lived.[4] But they were definitely not being called to *initial faith*. They were already believing in and walking with the one, true God who had set them apart from all the other nations to serve Him uniquely from their birth as a nation to the time of Jesus.

Stephen: Orthodox *before* Trusting Jesus

We learn from Stephen that Abraham, Isaac, and Jacob, along with Jacob's twelve sons, all believed in and walked with the God of Israel just as Abraham had done. While the *initial acceptance by God* of the main characters of the OT is *never* de-

---

[1] Cf., Rom. 7:7-25.

[2] Matt. 1:21; 2:6: John 1:11-12.

[3] John 3:3, 4, 14-16. Cf., also Lk. 1:13-17.

[4] John 3:19-21. Relate Matt. 3:2 to Matt. 4:17 and then both to Lk. 3:3-14.

scribed for the reader of the OT Scriptures, making me wonder whether such a concept is Biblically supportable, it is certain that they all knew God and had responded to His revelation to them. The record of their lives establishes this quite clearly. This approach, you might say, is the M.O., the *modus operandi*, of the OT writers. *They assumed a knowledge of the one, true God on the part of the persons being discussed and then focused upon their continuing faith in God and the relationship with Him that developed as they walked by faith.* And, of course, many who knew God never seem to develop a very dependent relationship upon Him at all.

> The OT focuses upon what is important to God: a walk that pleases Him.

When the NT speaks of Abraham's, of Isaac's, and of Jacob's inclusion in the kingdom when it is established at Jesus' return to earth, it verifies for us that Israel's forefathers had walked throughout their lives with the one, true God who had revealed Himself to them. Only the practically righteous, that is, only those who have walked with God, being dependent upon Him as they live their lives, can enter that future, earthly kingdom of Messiah.[1] They will enter it because they had such a life.

Stephen's little history lesson tells us what Stephen believed **before** he trusted in Jesus. He didn't believe in Jesus and then come to believe the OT history of the patriarchs' faith in the one, true God. He believed all this **before** he ever trusted in Jesus himself.

Now in addition to Abraham, Isaac, and Jacob, Stephen called the twelve patriarchs, each the head of one of the twelve tribes of Israel, *the forefathers* of the Jewish nation both physically

---

[1] E.g., Matt. 5:20; 7:21; Lk. 13:22-30.

and religiously. God affirmed that truth Himself over and over through the prophets of the OT.[1] The whole nation, according to Stephen's inspired history, was a believing nation. While Western Christianity generally throws the nation of Israel under the bus, God affirmed that they have always been His people,[2] called for a unique ministry of service for Him toward the rest of the world. They can't be thrown under the bus; they are driving the bus!

And the most important fact of all is that Stephen delivers his little history lesson in such a way that we are led to expect that the religious leaders to whom he was speaking also believed what he was detailing for them. If they did, and it is self-evidently true that they did, they had responded to God as their forefathers had and as Stephen had whom they were persecuting. The *spiritually responsive* Jewish leaders, who had up to this point rejected Jesus as their Messiah, were on the verge of putting to death Stephen. And Stephen had not only been a *spiritually responsive* Jew *before* Jesus came onto the scene but had also now been given eternal life by trusting in Jesus as his Messiah.

Saul, as we will discover, is the personification of both of these truths for us. He was divinely intended to represent *both* groups of people, *both* sides of this issue. His walk

> Being acceptable to God and being saved by Jesus are not the same thing.

with the God that he was believing in found approval with God *before* he ever met Jesus on the road to Damascus. This will be verified in our study as we let Saul speak for himself. After trusting in Jesus and receiving eternal life, he became the great-

---

[1] Acts 7:31-32.

[2] Cf., Hos. 12:9; 13:4; Hag. 2:5. Hosea wrote around 760 BC and Haggai around 520 BC.

est apostle of all. He nicely represents both groups of people.

While Stephen's opponents had rejected Jesus and had put Him to death, those facts do not negate the truth of their previously approved status before God. Both Saul and the religious leaders persecuting Stephen will become murderers, but everything they did, they did supposing that they were serving the one, true God, the God of Israel.[1] Did they have selfish motives mixed in with their service? Probably. But in that they are no different from many of us today.

Their walk of faith did not guarantee the correctness of their understanding or the propriety of their actions. The conclusions that they reached about Jesus and His Jewish followers seemed right to them, but actually those convictions led to their own ruin and to the nation's destruction. In reality they were opposing the God that they were seeking to serve. Yet their opposition to God and to His Messiah did not nullify the validity of their faith in and desire to serve the one, true God. A follower of the one, true God doesn't have to be always right for his faith to be genuine or even vita. We should all be glad of that fact, shouldn't we?

Stephen's defense affirms for us the spiritual life of the Jewish nation throughout its recorded history in the OT Scriptures. This includes Stephen's generation during the time of Jesus' ministry in the first century. Stephen was telling everyone that the Jews of the first century were already God's people *before* they accepted or rejected Jesus and His message.

Lastly, if we take Luke's introduction to his Gospel as inviolable and apply it to the Book of Acts as well, we are forced to accept the fact that someone in the chambers where the Sanhedrin met that day told Luke about the testimony that Stephen had

---

[1] Cf., John 16:1-2.

given. The first viable candidate, of course, is Saul since Luke was his traveling companion on his second missionary journey and on his trip to Rome as a prisoner. But it could have been any other person in that chamber as well.

Should this be taken for indirect confirmation by all those present during Stephen's trial that Stephen's little history was a truthful presentation of the facts? I think so. The Jewish religious leaders, confirmed by Stephen's own testimony to be part of God's people, were about to murder one of God's gifted servants. It wasn't the first time that such a thing had happen among the Jewish people. Nevertheless, the testimony stands firm: they were God's people who not only believed in Him but worshipped and served Him as well.

Chapter 3

Stephen's Denunciation

Stephen's denunciation of the religious leaders provides a huge correction to our theology if we are open to it. As it was pointed out in the last chapter, Stephen was dealing with his accusers and judges as though they were *spiritually responsive individuals*. (I'm trying to avoid the use of the term "believer" because it has become such a theologically loaded term that it no longer represents the Bible's use of it.) It must be observed that it was none other than God Himself who called the Jews in bondage in Egypt ~ every single one of them ~ His *first born*. Even the second generation, after forty years of wandering, would serve Him when they entered the Promised Land. By the use of a figure of speech called metonymy, Stephen declared that the whole nation of Israel in Egypt constituted the present nation's "forefathers"[1] since Abraham, Isaac, Jacob, and Jacob's twelve sons would have been long since dead by the time indicated in this passage.

The Spirit of God had been convicting the hearts of God's chosen people, the nation of Israel, for well over fifteen hundred years. *In no generation had obedience become the natural response of any of its people.* Stephen spoke to his accusers as though they were part of those who had *responded positively to God's revelation* (they would be called "believers" by us today). Yet he also de-

---

[1] Acts 7:17-19.

scribed them as living in opposition to God rather than living dependently upon Him. Although we've been taught that living in opposition to God is not possible for a true believer, Israel, identified by God Himself as His first-born son, did just that! Consequently, Israel shows us that God's *sons* can live rebellious lives. Listen carefully to Stephen's description of his accusers in Acts 7:51a:

> "You men, who are stiff-necked and uncircumcised in heart and ears, are always resisting the Holy Spirit . . ."

There are few people I suppose who have ever worked in the leadership structure of a Christian organization that have not witnessed the same characteristics among Christians that Stephen saw in the Jewish leaders in the first century. Being stiff-necked, uncircumcised in heart, and consistently resisting the conviction of the Spirit of God are characteristics that are true of every single person on planet Earth. Such characteristics are not unique to those who are *supposedly* the lost, unbelievers condemned to hell eternally.

Stephen's denunciation of the religious leaders, who were accusing him, leads us to believe that he saw the people, standing before him accusing him, as individuals who knew God and had responded to Him in their lives. If we analyze Stephen's next comments carefully, we can see his thinking process. He said,

> "... you are doing just as *your fathers* did. Which one of the prophets did *your fathers* not persecute? And they killed those who had previously announced the coming of the Righteous One, whose betrayers and murderers you have now become; *you who had received the law* as ordained by angels, *and yet did not keep it.*" (Acts 7:51b-53, emphases mine)

What a declaration! Stephen had just moments before described them as God's people who worshipped and served Him. Without rescinding that description, he also likened them to their forefathers who had persecuted the prophets sent to them. In persecuting him, they were doing the same thing that their forefathers had done.

While not all of God's prophets addressed His chosen nation, here Stephen is discussing only those that did. God Himself had declared this nation to be His own *sons* throughout their entire history recorded in the OT. And He sent His prophets to rebuke the sins of His *sons* and to warn them of the possibility of judgment at the hands of invading nations. But at all times the people of Israel, though divided into two kingdoms, continued to be related to God as *sons*. They were all part of His people and the sheep of His pasture.[1]

Study these writing prophets and mark down all the information that they give about the people to whom they were sent. And what exactly was the message they were given to deliver? What you will discover is the prophets were sent to God's chosen people in order to call them to repentance. They were sent to admonish the people of Israel, divided into two kingdoms while remaining one nation before God, to turn back to Him. The prophets were not sent to people that needed evangelizing in the modern sense of that term. *There is no evangelism undertaken anywhere in the OT toward Israel.* We must not expect God's people today to be any different in character,

> There are only revivals: God's messengers urging God's people to return to Him.

---

[1] Cf., Ps. 100:3. Notice that verse one identifies *the whole world* as God's people and the sheep of His pasture!

disposition, and propensity from the nation of Israel in the Old Testament.

Not only did the Israelites persecute the prophets God sent to them, a fact that Jesus retold in His *Parable of the Vineyard Workers* in Matthew 21:33-46, they actually killed some of them, another fact that Jesus confirmed in the same parable. Could "sons of God" act so wickedly, so wrongly? It is a fact that they have,[1] a fact that leads us to believe that they could still act just as badly in the first century when the Messiah finally appeared. This too Jesus confirmed to us in that same parable.

Stephen's denunciation of the religious leaders did not denote their eternal condemnation. It did signify their opposition to God because they were resisting the Holy Spirit whom God had previously set in their midst to lead them. Obviously, part of His leading ministry involved a convicting work to clarify the path of righteousness. But it must be noted that they had the capacity to resist the Spirit's leading, incurring God's judgment upon their present actions, not upon their future destiny.

---

[1] Cf., Isa. 1:2-4.

Chapter 4

Stephen's Death by Stoning

Saul's commitment to his Jewish faith led him to be involved in the execution of Stephen. We find Saul standing by watching the stoning as he held the cloaks of those who cast the stones. Saul cast one of the stones that condemned Stephen; the false witnesses cast the stones that executed him. And the same ire that is manifested by the religious leaders against Stephen finds a foothold in Saul's life as the Scriptures take so much care to warn its readers that it has the tendency to do.[1] Saul admitted to Luke that he was eaten up with anger over his Jewish brethren turning to faith in Jesus as their promised Messiah.[2] Luke described Saul's reaction this way:

> "Now Saul, *still breathing threats and murder* against the disciples of the Lord, went to the high priest, and asked for letters from him to the synagogues at Damascus, so that if he found any belonging to the Way, both men and women, he might bring them bound to Jerusalem." (Acts 9:1-2)

The reader gets the idea that Saul had become an agent of the Devil, taking on his character and purpose as he turned into a fire-breathing dragon, looking, before that future time of great distress had come, for those who had produced the Christ in order to destroy them.[3] So similarly, Saul sought out to destroy

---

[1] Cf., e.g., Prov. 22:24-25; 16:32.

[2] Acts 8:1-3.

[3] Cf., Rev. 12:3-4, 9, 13-17.

those who were targeted for no other reason than they had believed in Jesus as the promised Messiah.

Saul was looking for the Messiah along with most of the rest of the nation. His task as a Pharisee was to protect the people from imposters and heretics by using the OT Scriptures as the means for discerning who might be leading the people astray.[1] The irony is that he actually became the heretic that he was trying to guard the people against. He thought the new Messianic Jews were heretics for *accepting* Jesus as the promised Messiah. But in God's eyes he had become the heretic for *rejecting* Jesus as the Messiah.

> Saul's defense of the *status quo* became an affront to God.

We must all be aware lest we join him in opposing God even though we might be, like Saul had been, zealous for following God faithfully.

Saul was, I believe, responding to *the consensus theology of his day*. Since those in leadership and power were not committing themselves to follow Jesus in faith, he received their view of the circumstances and *supposed* them to be correct. He followed their lead but eventually found himself opposing God.

Now he would have to overcome his *theological and unbiblical entrenchment* and become open to God's continuing revelation that was coming through His own Son. It would not be an easy task to change previously held convictions thought to be correct.

---

[1] Cf., Deut. 13:1-4.

Chapter 5

The Impact upon Saul's Life

Because Saul's encounter with Stephen must have been one of the most powerful *goads* God used in his life, it is not surprising to find motifs that arose in that ill-handled conflict become themes that Saul would use to instruct other followers of Jesus after his call to apostleship. The more Paul became like Jesus,[1] interestingly enough, the more he would become like Stephen because Stephen had already become so much like Jesus himself. As Saul *lived by faith* in the empowerment of the Spirit of God, he displayed both the wisdom[2] and the grace[3] that were also so evident in Stephen's life.[4]

In like manner, *the fullness of the Spirit* that characterized Stephen[5] must have greatly impressed Saul. He later penned the only command in the NT by which every believer is required to be filled with the Spirit of the living God.[6] It is only because Paul's explanation of it has been removed from its historical and literary contexts that there is so much misunderstanding over the phenomenon. A careful meditation on Stephen's character and actions in Acts six and seven would correct most of that.

---

[1] Cf., 2Cor. 3:18; 1Cor. 11:1; Gal. 4:19.

[2] 1Cor. 1:18—2:5.

[3] 2Cor. 12:7-9.

[4] Acts 6:8, 10.

[5] Acts 6:5.

[6] Eph. 5:18. See also 1Cor. 2:1-5.

Because Paul had already given a careful exposition of it in Eph. 3:14-17, he could simply refer to it as the filling of the Spirit in Eph. 5:18.

And on the negative side of the ledger, Stephen's accusation against the religious leaders, describing them as people who, like their forefathers in the faith, were always *resisting* the Holy Spirit,[1] must have made a deep impression on Saul. Later he would warn Christians against both *quenching* the Holy Spirit[2] and *grieving* the Holy Spirit,[3] two terms that seem to convey the same concept as *resisting* the Holy Spirit. In light of these several passages, it is only because of a theological bias that one would be led to reject the idea that man has the capacity to resist God's overtures toward him. He clearly has that ability, and may be unwittingly exercising it even as he is attempting to follow what he thinks God is requiring.

This ability to resist the Holy Spirit was manifested in Saul as well as in the religious leaders who condemned and executed Stephen. This ability is evident in the fact that God had used the goad against Saul several times. When Jesus asked him, "(Is it) hard, Saul, to kick against the goads?"[4] He used the plural for goad. There was more than one whack on the backside of Saul by God. The goads would continue until Saul was ready to *stop resisting* the revelation that God was giving him through each follower of Jesus that he was persecuting or until his heart became fully set in its opposition.[5] No one but God seems to know when that point is.

---

[1] Acts 7:51.

[2] 1Thess. 5:19.

[3] Eph. 4:30.

[4] Acts 26:14.

[5] Cf., Acts 14:16; Rom. 1:24, 26, 28.

The fact that Saul gave into the goads should not lead us to conclude that everyone always does the same. Some never come to their senses even in the face of God's repeated goading. And soon God stops goading! Romans chapter one establishes the truth that there are people who know God[1] but who move away from Him.[2] As a result God gives them over to the corrupt lifestyle of their choosing.[3]

This voluntary separation from God and His will affects their ability to properly understand life.[4] As long as God is goading, there is hope of figuring out life and our place in it. Saul needed more than one whack on the back to pull the plough in the right direction. So may we.

Saul's lessons from his encounter with Stephen didn't end there. Surely his own *anger,* directed both toward Stephen at that time and later toward other Messianic Jews wherever he could find them, must have been a point of shame for some time. Maybe this is the reason that he dealt with anger and malice in his letter to the Ephesian believers.[5] It is a very painful admission to recognize that you have been an effective tool of Satan at times even though you thought you were being so faithful to God at those exact times. It hurts. It really does.

Then, of course, we have the issue of Stephen's *calling on the name of the Lord.*[6] Surely Stephen's act of calling on the name of the Lord, along with that phrase's OT roots,[7] became the source of Saul's concept of that phenomenon. He used it to describe

---

[1] Rom. 1:21.

[2] Rom. 1:22-23.

[3] Rom. 1:24, 26.

[4] Rom. 1:21, 28.

[5] Eph. 4:25-32.

[6] Acts 7:59.

[7] Cf., Gen. 4:26; 12:7-8; 21:32-33; etc. Not once is it used for obtaining "salvation" in the traditional sense of that term today.

how the Jews, living in the future just before their salvation comes through the returning Messiah, will call upon the name of the Lord for their physical deliverance (salvation).[1] This deliverance may come through physical death as it did in Stephen's case. Or it may come through Jesus' intervention into the circumstances of the person calling upon his name. When the Jewish people, alive at the end of the Great Tribulation, call upon His name, Jesus will return from heaven and save the nation from her enemies.[2] This is the Biblical meaning of "calling on the name of the Lord" in Rom. 10:9-13.

Calling on the name of the Lord is not the means of escaping hell and of going to heaven. It concerns seeking Jesus' intervention in this life. The reason for the wide-spread misunderstanding of this phrase is that we read into the term *salvation* what we have been taught theologically rather than allowing the Biblical context to determine its meaning. Salvation is not a reference to a heavenly destiny anywhere in the book of Romans or in the rest of the Bible for that matter.

And finally, Stephen's actual *vision of Jesus* standing at the right hand of God's throne might be the first seeds of Paul's belief that Jesus was **not** on His own throne ruling yet. He was on the Father's throne waiting for His coming time to rule. That time will not begin until He returns to the earth after the Great Tribulation.[3] He is currently interceding as the Great High Priest[4] for His saints on earth.[5]

Saul may have thought he was serving God as he put Ste-

---

[1] Joel 2:28-32.

[2] E.g., Lk. 1:68-75.

[3] Cf., Matt. 25:31.

[4] Cf., Heb. 3:1.

[5] Cf., Heb. 7:25.

phen to death;[1] he may even have done so with a good con-science.[2] But to kick against the goads described the ox's literal kick against the rod being used to prod the animal along. It was used for the lazy ox which didn't want to pull the plough at all, for the ox which, having a mind of its own, tended to pull the plough wide of the intended furrow, and for the ox that needed direction when it was time to make adjustments, turning as the shape or boundary of the field required. God had an intended plough line set up, and Saul may have been pulling wide of that mark. He needed to be goaded to come into alignment with God's intended plans to plough the field. God also had a pre-scribed field with a prescribed shape and boundary that re-quired adjustments to be made to plough the whole field but not beyond it. Saul may have needed some coercion to make the proper adjustments, turning at the place God was indicating by the goad applied to his backside. But it is certain that Saul did not need the goading because he was lazy![3] Realignment issues in the ministry are so common. It is uncommon not to have one.

It should be self-evidently true that *Saul had already been en-gaged as an ox for ploughing God's field of ministry **before** he trusted Jesus on the road to Damascus. Jesus was goading him **to continue to pull the plough** and to make the proper adjustments or turns as the field required!* The point is Saul had already been enlisted for ser-vice for God *before* he ever trusted in Jesus. That previous ser-vice essentially required him, as a diligent Pharisee,[4] to follow the pattern for ministry that Ezra had established for himself over four hundred years before the time of Saul:

---

[1] Cf., John 16:1-2.

[2] Acts 24:14-16.

[3] Cf., Gal. 1:13-14, 23; Acts 9:1-2.

[4] Cf., Phil. 3:5 and the phrase "as to the Law, a Pharisee."

"For Ezra had set his heart to *study* the law of the Lord, and to *practice* it, and to *teach* His statutes and ordinances in Israel." (Ezra 7:10)

It was hard, but not impossible, to kick against the goads of God! Each one of us manifest that truth daily in our lives. God is trying to speak to us to guide us into the path He wants us to walk, but for a variety of reasons, we stubbornly refuse to listen to Him. Each kick is an act of personal defiance. Although Saul was kicking against God's goads, yet what he was doing he was doing in ignorance.[1] God was about to uniquely enlighten him.[2]

---

[1] 1Tim. 1:13-14.

[2] Acts 9:3-6, 10-16, 19-22.

Chapter 6

Saul Trusts in Jesus

Saul could not get over his encounter with Stephen. It was one of several *goads* that the Lord Jesus used to draw Saul to Himself. But the confrontation with Stephen may have been the first, really troubling one that he had to face. Nevertheless, the anger that Stephen occasioned during his trial and stoning continued to burn within Saul. He became more proactive, unrelenting, and increasingly harsh, even violent, in his opposition to his Jewish brethren who had come to believe that Jesus was indeed God's promised Messiah.

In Luke's record of the details of Saul's encounter with the resurrected Jesus on the road to Damascus, he began by saying,

> "Now Saul *still breathing threats and murder* against the disciples of the Lord, …" (Acts 9:1, emphasis mine)

Just as Stephen's immediate opponents were not able to cope with his wisdom or with the spirit in which he presented and defended his views,[1] Saul obviously had a difficult time doing the same thing. It must have been unsettling to see a common Jewish layman stand against his highly educated contemporaries with such grace, power, and wisdom. He must have felt a bewildering astonishment, mixed, of course, with a great deal of aggravation. After all, Stephen was another unanswerable op-

---

[1] Acts 6:10.

ponent, like the ones the Sanhedrin had experienced earlier when it confronted Peter and John after they had healed a lame man at the door of the temple. In the case of Peter and John, the Sanhedrin recognized that the cogent defense by these two uneducated fishermen could be explained only by recognizing that their time with Jesus had made an incredible difference in them.[1]

Stephen had spent time with Jesus too, only his time with Jesus had been undertaken in a completely spiritual fashion after Jesus had ascended back into heaven. He spent time with Jesus in the same way that you and I have to approach it today. We should expect no less an impact upon us than what Stephen experienced in his devotional times with Jesus.

This new belief had to be silenced. So, Saul committed himself to do just that. Luke explained the steps Saul undertook to bring an end to this growing, new persuasion called the Way:

> "Saul . . . went to the high priest, and asked for letters from him *to the synagogues at Damascus* so that if he found any belonging to the Way, both men and women, he might bring them bound to Jerusalem." (Acts 9:1-2, emphasis mine)

Saul was given the authority to search the synagogues for Jews who had received Jesus as the Messiah. Excommunication from the synagogue over Jesus had been practiced since the time of Jesus' personal ministry.[2] But, as far as the Biblical text goes, the physical persecution being added to the excommunication was relatively new.[3] But Saul was not trying to stamp out all the cults in the land of Israel. His full focus was upon Jews who were, in his opinion, disrupting and even abandoning the traditions

---

[1] Acts 4:13.

[2] John 9:22, 34.

[3] Cf., Acts 4-5. But it was a fulfillment of Jesus' words (John 16:1-2).

handed down for centuries[1] by believing that the Messiah had come. These Jews that Saul was weeding out from the synagogues had to be silenced before others were misled into following them in their error, or so Saul must have reasoned.

It came about that in the process of punishing his Jewish brethren for believing in Jesus, Saul had a surprise encounter with Jesus on the road to Damascus. According to Luke's narrative of the story he obtained from Saul as he later traveled with him on his missionary journeys, an incredibly bright light suddenly shone around Saul and his traveling companions, apparently causing them to fall to the ground. A voice was heard speaking in a Hebrew dialect,[2] and Saul, who could speak Hebrew, asked who it was who was speaking to him. And Jesus clearly identified Himself as the voice speaking to Saul.[3] Then He told Saul to continue his journey into Damascus, and there he would find out what God had in store for him.[4]

> Ananias' task was to commission Saul for further service.

After a couple of days, Jesus appeared to Ananias and sent him to Saul to give him further instructions. While these new instructions were not very detailed, they did give Saul the big picture of what God had in mind for him. God explained to Ananias:

> "Go, for he [Saul] **is** *a choice vessel* to Me, *to bear My name* before the Gentiles and kings and the sons of Israel; for I will show him how much he must suffer for My name's sake." (Acts 9:15-16, my translation, bracket, and emphases)

---

[1] Cf., Acts 6:14. This was part of the skewed testimony against Stephen that Saul may have heard in the high council chambers that day.

[2] Acts 26:14.

[3] Acts 26:15.

[4] Acts 9:1-9.

Saul, who had rejected Jesus as the Messiah up until this point, was being described to Ananias as *a choice vessel* in God's own evaluation of him. In God's opinion, then, Saul had *already* been a special instrument in His hands; he had *already* been *an excellent servant* for God however presently misguided he may have been.

The point that must not be missed is the tense of the verb Luke used here. It is a present tense, denoting Saul's present, spiritual condition at the time God spoke to Ananias. At that moment Saul was already a choice vessel! Jesus didn't tell Ananias that Saul would eventually become an excellent minister for Him. He told Ananias that Saul was already such a person. He was already proven, a vessel of honor in the service of God.

What God wanted to do was to *change his calling*; He wanted to enlist him into a *new ministry* to better serve Him as he moved forward in his life. He would now proclaim the very same message that he had been trying to stamp out. *Since Saul was the cream of the crop in his day, God chose him for a task that needed just such a man as he was.* This is a perfect portrayal of the Biblical doctrine of election. Saul with his maturity, experience, and giftedness is chosen by God to use them in a new calling.

> To be a deterrent to God one only needs to reject the new revelation or the new illumination that He is giving.

Saul was trained; he knew the OT Scriptures as well as anyone; he was zealous for God; and he lived out his faith daily. He was a proven minister already! So, he was the perfect *choice* for further ministry responsibilities.

Because Saul was a *choice* or *excellent servant already*, God changed his previous calling, a point I alluded to earlier under the goading metaphor and will demonstrate from Paul's writings a little later, without interrupting his service for Him. Saul was being given new revelation that God expected him to receive so that he could expand the service he was already giving to Him.

As we carefully read Luke's narrative of Saul's Damascus road experience, we discover some particulars describing Ananias' purpose in going to Saul. In verses seventeen and eighteen, we find that Ananias was to give Saul his sight back, to give Saul the Holy Spirit, and to baptize him[1] so that he could fulfill his divine commission for service, noted in verses six and fifteen.

Acts nine is pretty clear to most readers. There really isn't a lot of debate over the facts presented here. This is the time when and the place where Saul first comes to believe in Jesus. Nothing could be simpler, right? Well, everything would be extremely simple if we did not bring a boat load of theological assumptions to this passage that are not found in it or supported by it.

What are some of those assumptions? For simplicity's sake I will give a few bullet points listing some of the assumptions that are usually brought to a text such as this one.

- Everyone had to believe in *a coming Messiah* to be *saved* from hell (wrong on two counts)
- Belief in *a coming Messiah* had to result in belief in Jesus as **the** *Messiah* for forgiveness of sins to be granted (wrong on two counts)
- Justification and salvation are *related issues* that occur at *the point of initial faith* (wrong on two counts)
- Justification involves two things: the *forgiveness* of all sins (past, present, and future), and *the gift of perfect righteous-*

---

[1] Acts 9:17-18.

ness (wrong on both counts)

- *Hell* is escaped and *heaven* obtained at *initial faith* (wrong on three counts)

So, in this episode in the life of Saul, many *assume* that what is taking place here is **both** his justification by God and his salvation by Jesus.

It is *assumed* that all of Saul's life up to this point was of a *legal* sort, completely external in nature without any internal reality.

It is *assumed* that Saul was waiting for the Messiah, supposedly, to provide a payment needed to obtain forgiveness from God. Consequently, if he, or anyone else, rejected Jesus, he would not obtain the payment for his sins. Without that payment, he was sure to spend an eternity in hell, or so it has been *assumed*.

In addition, it is *assumed* that Saul needed the perfect righteousness that would be given to him from Christ Jesus Himself the moment he trusted in Jesus as his Savior. With this new righteousness, it is *assumed* that he would be saved forever from hell and assured of a heavenly destiny. Since no one can be *saved* from hell who does not believe in the one name given under heaven for that specific benefit, no one can be saved (or justified or forgiven) who does not believe in Jesus.[1]

With Saul's rejection of Jesus he had to have been eternally condemned. *That* is the most basic and pertinent *assumption* of all.

Are these assumptions Biblically accurate? Or are they theological deviations from what the Bible actually teaches?

---

[1] Acts 4:12.

What if we were to find that initial faith was *never, not once,* called justification? Would that affect what you believe?

What if we can ascertain that justification does not occur at the same time as salvation? Would that change your view of justification and salvation?

What if we, furthermore, discover that justification is related to redemption, propitiation, and reconciliation and all four of these issues deal with a person's *walk* with God rather than to the moment he *supposedly* first believed in God? Would that alter what you believe?

Further, *what if* we uncover the truth that salvation is a reference to at least five different things, none of which *explicitly* describes a deliverance from hell? Would you still think that believing in Jesus saves a person from hell?

And finally, *what if* we discover that a person does not need a once-for-all-obtained *righteous standing* before God in order to be acceptable to Him?

What if we learn that God invites all men to come to Him just as they are, and that He receives them that way without any need for a righteous standing or for a once-for-all forgiveness of all of their sins?

If these things could be demonstrated from the Scriptures, as I have done in my previous book, *The Prodigal Paradigm, the Bible's real storyline*, and could be illustrated in the life of a Biblical person such as Saul, as I intend to do in this book, would they impact what you believe and communicate? Or will you continue believing what has become so familiar to you after all these years even though it may be erroneous? We must remember that even the apostle Paul said that if we ever teach something that is not true, we become false witnesses of God and liars.[1] I don't expect God to take that very lightly, do you? And don't forget: James, Jesus' half-brother said the same thing before Paul did.

Yes, I am suggesting that we may need to veer away from what we have been taught in the past. Could you or would you do it? Each one of us will give an account of how faithfully he has carried out the stewardship of God's Word entrusted to him.[2] We will not be held accountable for how faithfully we adhered to the historical theologies that have become the consensus plumb line for belief within Christianity. What we find in God's Word ought to trump every doctrine of man.[3] Are we resting our eternal judgment upon what others have concluded the Bible says or upon what we have confirmed the Bible really does teach?

It is clear that Saul first believed in Jesus somewhere in his road-to-Damascus experience. But what is not clear, even if it is fiercely and tenaciously held onto as an incontrovertible fact, is whether Saul was doomed for hell up until the time he believed in Jesus. To state the dilemma bluntly: "Could Saul's faith and spiritual walk have been approved by and pleasing to God *before* he ever trusted in Jesus?" Once the Bible becomes our guide and highest authority, that question will be surprisingly easy to answer.

A follow up question may be, "If Saul had remained in his unbelief relative to Jesus being the Messiah, would his spiritual condition, assuming, for the sake of discussion, that it had been acceptable to God already, have been nullified and his eternal

---

[1] Cf., 1Cor. 15:15.

[2] 1Cor. 4:1-2; 2Tim. 1:13-14; 2:1-7.

[3] Matt. 15:6, 9.

life forfeited?"[1]

Is there some unwritten law that forces us to conclude that in the first century every believer in God had to believe on Jesus before he died?

Was every believer in the one, true God at the time of Christ forced by some logical or fateful necessity to believe in Jesus when Jesus presented Himself as an object of faith?

Or could a person who genuinely believed in God and followed Him the best he could still reject Jesus as the Messiah without any eternal consequences resulting?

We must now pursue answers to these questions. Needless to say, this is the place that our study gets really interesting! The reader must remember that Saul, who becomes the apostle Paul, is the living example, who is confirmed by the inspired Word of God, that the historic Christian doctrine of soteriology is based upon man's theology rather than the Bible. That is the reason our study gets interesting.

---

[1] Just to be clear, I have used the terms saved and salvation in their traditionally accepted, historical sense according to orthodox Christianity, namely, that of being saved from hell and obtaining heaven in hell's place. How does one get this salvation? By believing in Jesus (Acts 16:30-31). It is my conviction that such a meaning cannot be supported from the Scriptures, not even from Acts 16:30-31. Salvation has nothing to do with going to heaven or escaping hell.

Section Two

What Saul Said About Himself

Chapter 7

Saul's Personal Testimony
Before a Jewish Mob

We have to move ahead now almost 20 years in Saul's life. At this point he had ministered for Jesus for nearly two decades, spending a good portion of that time on the mission field. Now he had returned to Jerusalem where he had agreed to put Stephen to death by stoning and where he had ravaged the church by imprisoning Jewish men and women who had believed in Jesus. Ironically enough, he was arrested by Roman soldiers in order to keep him from being killed by a mob incensed that he was now preaching what he had once persecuted. This enraged Jewish mob accused him of preaching …

> "to all men everywhere against our people, and the Law, and this [Jewish] place [of worship]." (Acts 21:28, brackets mine)

These were the very same accusations that had been leveled against Stephen earlier as he preached Jesus.[1] And Saul had to have been concerned by the fact that these accusations had been sufficient for him and the other Jewish religious leaders to sentence Stephen to death. How could he expect a different treatment or a less severe or final fate than Stephen had received? He knew how easily excited his countrymen were emotionally. Would their rage demand less than his rage had demanded

---

[1] Acts 6:13-14.

twenty years earlier?

In this little episode we learn several biographical facts about Saul. First, he was multi-lingual.[1] He spoke Greek, Aramaic, and Hebrew, and most likely Latin as well, being a Roman citizen. It is natural to suspect that he was a highly educated man, a fact validated for us later in the Book of Acts.[2] But this multilingual facility probably should not be pressed too far since Saul chose to speak to the Jewish mob in Hebrew when the common language among those inhabiting the territories of the former empire of Alexander the Great was Greek. Hence, most people of Saul's day were probably bi-lingual at least, if not tri-lingual.

Saul, a Typical Jew, with a Typical, Jewish Faith

As we look at his defense before this Jewish mob, we ought to analyze each point that Saul used in his defense. As he began to address the mob, hoping to give a witness to his faith in Jesus, he identified himself to his audience, saying,

"I am a Jew . . ." (Acts 22:3)

What does that mean? It is natural, I believe, to see in this statement a declaration of religious significance as well as ethnicity. Over two hundred times, scattered throughout the OT, we can find the phrase "the God of Israel." The one, true God was the God of Israel. And Saul will leave no doubt about his relationship with Him if we will let him speak freely.

> God was the God of the Jewish people and, therefore, the God of Saul as well.

We also learn that Saul was born in Tarsus of Cilicia, but he

---

[1] Acts 22:2.

[2] Acts 26:24.

was brought up in Jerusalem.[1] I remember reading somewhere about a Jewish epigram that was well-known in ancient Israel. It said, and I must paraphrase here, "If you want to be rich, live in Galilee; if you want to be spiritual, live in Jerusalem." Saul moved to Jerusalem to be educated at the feet of Gamaliel.[2] While there is not a lot of information on the historical figure known as Gamaliel in the *Book of Acts* (and within Jewish literature there are several persons named Gamaliel), what is given in Acts 5 and Acts 22 is presumed to be true since it was written under the guidance of the Spirit of God.[3]

Gamaliel's High View of God

If Acts 5:38-39 is any indication of the wisdom that Saul received as he sat under his spiritual mentor, he came away with a very high view of the God of Israel. This high view came from His self-revelation. In the advice that Gamaliel gave to the Sanhedrin about the arrested apostles, he said,

> "And so in the present case I say to you, stay away from these men and let them alone, for if this plan or action should be of men, it will be overthrown; but *if it is of God*, you will not be able to overthrow them; or else *you may even be found fighting against God.*" (emphases mine)

Gamaliel was telling the religious leaders that plans of men eventually come to nothing; but the plans of God cannot be overthrown. That the apostles were released from jail in a way that no one could explain except that God be taken into account can be attributed to his warning to "stay away from these men

---

[1] Acts 22:3.

[2] ibid. Cf., Acts 26:4.

[3] 2Pet. 1:21; 3:14-16.

and let them alone." The God of Israel was the only God to be taken seriously; He alone was the true God. That was what *all the religious leaders believed* and that is the reason they took Gamaliel's advice. Believing in this sort of God, and being responsible for the spiritual climate of this God's people, they naturally sought advice about the best way to serve Him.

Men in the OT, that is, men up to the time Jesus set foot on the stage of human history, found approval by responding to the God who was meeting them in the midst of their circumstances. This is what the author of the Book of Hebrews *explicitly* taught when he said,

> "For *by it* [faith] the men of old gained *approval* [from God]... and *without faith it is impossible to please Him* for he who comes to God must believe that He is, and that He is a rewarder of those who seek Him." (Heb. 11:2, 6, emphases and brackets mine)

It must be noted that there is no mention here of a Messiah in whom these men had to believe. They didn't have to believe in His virgin birth, His coming, His death for their sins, or His resurrection. They simply needed to believe two things: 1.) that God existed; and 2.) that He rewarded each person who sought Him. Such people, the Scripture says, were pleasing to God. How could Saul, being the Jew that he was, come short of this standard in his fervent defense of his faith? It is difficult for anyone to be comfortable denying Saul's spiritual relationship with God in light of this simple, but Scriptural, two-point plumb line. If Reformed theology, considered the orthodox plumb line by many, didn't demand more, neither would we.

Gamaliel's High View of Scripture

As he continued his defense before this angry mob, Saul further confessed that he was educated strictly according to the law of his Jewish forefathers. While Gamaliel, it is generally thought, was of the Hillel camp which was supposed to be more open to oral traditions, Saul says that he "adhered to the strictness of the Jewish Law."[1] So whatever oral tradition he believed, it did not lessened his fervor for or his commitment to what was written in the Jewish Scriptures. Consequently, when he wrote 2Tim. 3:16-17, he was only consistently propagating, now under the inspiration of the Spirit of God, the view of the Scriptures he had accepted since childhood. Those verses proclaim that . . .

> "*All Scripture is inspired by God* and is profitable for teaching, for rebuke, for correction, for training in righteousness; that the man of God may be adequate, equipped for every good work."

Saul knew the OT Scriptures and the fact that the phrase "the word of the Lord" (or some equivalent) is used nearly two thousand times in them. That canon of writings was from God, Saul firmly believed, and it detailed how a person could live a life that God would accept. Saul was correct in his thinking. He knew that his obedience, for it to be pleasing to God, had to flow from *a vital faith* such as the one he had observed in Abraham, his forefather, in David, the greatest king Israel ever had, in Daniel, one of God's chosen prophets during Israel's darkest hours in the OT and especially in Moses, the great law giver, whose law was intended to encourage a faith walk that resulted in life (in the sense of a vital relationship with God) to the obedient for his obedience.

So now not only was Saul taught a high view of God from Gamaliel, he also had learned to have a high view of Scripture. Consequently, we find Saul challenging his disciples to protect

---

[1] ibid.

the revelation that they had received from God from any change or loss. He gave these commands to his closest disciples in his closing days:

> *Retain* the standard of sound words which you have heard from me, in the faith and love which are in Christ Jesus. *Guard,* through the Holy Spirit who dwells in us, the treasure which has been entrusted to you." (2Tim. 1:13-14, emphases mine)

Saul clung to the OT all his life; he considered it inspired revelation from God, legislating a lifestyle that God would readily commend. He was correct on all counts.

Saul's Zeal for God

Saul described his whole life from his youth and his early religious training to his adult life as a Pharisee as "being zealous for God." He naturally became a very zealous defender of his faith. Being well grounded in the OT history of God's repeated intervention in the life of the nation and in His victory over all the gods of all the other nations, Saul learned from his childhood that the God of Israel had proven conclusively that He was the one, true God and that there was no other.

This was the God that Saul believed in. This was the God he sought to please in everything he did. This was the object of his unshakable faith even *before* he trusted in Jesus. To find fault in Saul's beliefs or in his walk with the one, true God can be done only by circular reasoning, supposing that a rejection of Jesus must indicate an inadequate trust in God. If that same circular reasoning was applied to every Christian who refused to receive any new insights from God's word, where would that lead us?

Jesus was God's new revelation. He was sent to God's chosen nation to offer to fulfill God's promises and covenants given in the OT. The fulfillment of these promises and covenants would bring to a close God's plan for the earth. *That plan involved God's righteous rule being set up on the earth through human mediators who would represent and rule for God.* Israel refused the new revelation, and, thereby, postponed the establishment of God's rule upon this earth like it is enacted in the heavens (Matt. 6:10).

Saul clearly explained that *the zeal* that he began to feel as a young boy sitting at the feet of Gamaliel was *the same zeal* that "this mob" had, a mob who wanted to see him dead. But Saul took his comparison a step further when he said,

> Saul and the entire crowd of men seeking his life shared the same zeal for the same God.

"[I am] *being zealous for God just as you all* [the mob that sought his death] *are today.*" (Acts 22:3, brackets and emphases mine)

No one could understand the zeal that was driving this mob better than Saul. That zeal had led him to agree to the killing of Stephen twenty years earlier, and that same zeal was motivating this angry mob to kill Saul now. The object of the zeal was the same in both the mob and in Saul: the God of Israel. The intent of the zeal was the same in both: to defend and protect the revelation given by the God of Israel. These are the obvious facts that the Scriptures set before us.

But while Saul affirmed that he had been zealous for God his whole life, that really isn't the point he wanted to make here. Rather, the further step he took was to compare the zeal for God he had possessed *from his youth to this present moment* with the mob's zeal! He was not only comparing the past zeal he had *before* trusting in Jesus to the mob's present zeal for God. He was more precisely comparing His *present zeal for God after* having believed in and having served Jesus for two decades to their present zeal for God.[1]

The only difference is one had the benefit of God's progressive revelation and the blessings that flowed upon those who receive that revelation.

> Zeal for God *before* faith in Jesus and zeal for God *after* believing in Jesus were all the same for Saul.

This comparison of *zeals forces* the student of Scripture to re-think both Saul's spiritual condition from his youth onward as well as that of the mob that wanted to kill Saul. But Saul's zeal was not better, purer, or more pleasing to God after trusting in Jesus than it had been before he had trusted in Jesus. And the mob's present zeal for God, although they had rejected Jesus, was not less pleasing to God than Saul's zeal was as a Christian. That is what the text means. And while this zeal might not be in accordance with the latest revelation of God, it was still a divinely pleasing zeal.

> If Saul's zeal was that of a follower of the one, true God, then the zeal of the mob must be seen in exactly the same way.

While one had more light than the others, all had the same intention: to obey and glorify the God of Israel in their every decision.

In Saul's defense to the mob he was trying to proclaim his

---

[1] The finite verb is ειμι (translated "I am"), having four participles describe (or limit) it in four ways. Saul was saying, "I *am* a Jew, *having been born* (perfect participle, denoting a point in the past previous to the time of the main verb) . . . *having been brought up* (perfect participle, denoting a process in the past that came to its end with abiding results) . . . *having been educated* (perfect participle, denoting a process in the past that reached its goal with abiding results) under Gamaliel, and *being* (present participle, denoting a present description at the time of the main verb which is also in the present tense) *zealous for God* as he stood before the mob.

innocence. He was trying to tell this Jewish mob that he agreed with them in worshipping and serving the one, true God. This he said plainly, concisely, and poignantly when he identified himself as "a Jew." He really needed to say nothing else for the audience he was addressing.

He then told them of his experience on the road to Damascus. He identified the one who appeared to him in that light as Jesus. The mob listened as he told of his miraculous healing and of his return to Jerusalem to worship God in the temple, *demonstrating by that action no change from his former beliefs about God.*

The mob cried out for his death only when he told them of his vision from God. In that vision God had warned him to depart from Jerusalem because his testimony would not be accepted there. God, the mob's God don't forget, had commanded Saul to go to the Gentiles with the news about Jesus! Only upon that disclosure did the mob want his blood. Their antipathy toward Gentiles was more significant in determining their response than the possibility that Jesus might be their Messiah.[1]

Can a person have a zeal for the one, true God that resulted in an obedient lifestyle lived by faith, and yet be unpleasing to Him? The only way that this mob's zeal for God, and Saul's zeal along with theirs, can be set aside is for it to be arbitrarily described as something essentially less than what God says it is.

Saul's Commission to Serve

When Saul responded to the voice buried in the bright light, he asked, *"What shall I do,* Lord?"[2] To his question the answer came back,

---

[1] Acts 22:3-22.
[2] Acts 22:10.

"Arise and go on into Damascus; and there you will be told of all that has been appointed for you *to do*." (Acts 22:10)

Notice that, from Saul's question and Jesus' answer to it, it is clear that the focus or purpose of this encounter is entirely upon what Saul was "to do." *This extraordinary episode in his life was God's divine recruitment of Saul for the work of the ministry.* And all of this would seem very strange if Saul was not a mature follower at the time. If a neophyte is not to be chosen for the office of elder,[1] surely for the office of an apostle, especially one being sent throughout the Gentile world, a neophyte would be completely inappropriate.

The point is simply this: *Saul may have been a new believer in Jesus, but he wasn't a newcomer to faith in God.* He was a seasoned veteran who had immersed himself in the OT Scriptures, obeyed those Scriptures to God's complete satisfaction, and taught them to others so that they too could love God as God wanted them to do.[2] Saul was, in short, the epitome of the man God wanted all His children to be.

As a result, God gave him the privilege to serve in a new capacity. He had been serving God as a Pharisee. Now God was calling him to be an apostle of Jesus.

It is obvious that Luke meant his reader to understand that the Jesus who spoke to Saul from heaven was the same person Stephen said he saw "standing at the right hand of God" in heaven.[3] What a chilling experience that must have been for Saul. He could not cope with the power, grace, and wisdom of

---

[1] 1Tim. 3:6. Translating νεοφυτον as a "new convert" may miss Paul's point of not placing a novice, one with more zeal than mature discernment, in the position of spiritual leadership.

[2] Cf., Deut. 6:4-9; 7:9; John 14:21. Maybe this is the reason he penned 1Tim. 1:5.

[3] Acts 7:55.

Stephen who, just before his illegal stoning, identified the man standing by the throne of God in heaven as Jesus. Now this same Jesus condescended to appear to Saul in a bright light shining from heaven. Did He now come in judgment? Surely Saul was guilty of partaking in the killing of Jesus' disciple, Stephen. Or did He come for some other reason?

Ananias only exacerbated Saul's fear when he told him that the Jesus that had appeared to him in the bright light was the one who had sent him. If you miss the divine humor in the passage, let me explain it to you. Saul fell to the ground and was blinded at the first encounter he had with Jesus. Now Ananias warned Saul that if he hurt him or tried to imprisoned him, the same Jesus who had so overwhelmed him on the road to Damascus, had sent him, and would not hesitate to defend him. So, Saul, Ananias confidently warned, you should be very prudent in your response to the Messianic Jew standing before you!

Jesus did not appear to Saul to judge or condemn him. *He appeared to him to illumine him and expand his present ministry.* Just as pastors today may be *called* from one church to another in order to continue his ministry to a larger, broader audience, so Saul was being *called* from one ministry to another for the same reason. Because he was such a ***choice*** man of God already, he was ***eminently qualified*** for this new calling.[1]

Saul, a Second-Generation Pharisee

As Saul continued his defense before the mob, his next declaration should have stopped the agitators in their tracks given

---

[1] This is the meaning of the Greek terms that are generally misunderstood and mistranslated as elect/election/select/selection/chosen. Dr. C. Gordon Olson has demonstrated this, I believe, convincingly in his revised book, *Beyond Calvinism and Arminianism*. Global Gospel Publishers, 221 Farley Branch Drive, Lynchburg, Virginia, 24502.

the high esteem in which the Pharisees were held by all. Saul challenged the throng with these words:

"I am a Pharisee, a son of a Pharisee . . ." (Acts 23:6)

Not only had he been raised from his early youth to have a zeal for God, but in his adult life he had become a Pharisee, a guardian of the Holy Scriptures. Not only was he a "Jew" like they were; not only was he "zealous for God" like they were; He was also a Pharisee, someone who had dedicated his life to the study, defense, and propagation of the Jewish faith. Today we would compare Saul to a seminary faculty member who chaired both the Biblical Exposition Department because of his thorough knowledge of the Bible and the Missions Department because of his practical experience in propagating and defending his Biblical faith.

But Saul's spiritual condition is not exhausted by those descriptive terms. He was not only a Pharisee, he . . .

"lived as a Pharisee according to the strictest sect of our religion." (Acts 26:5, emphasis mine)

He took his faith very seriously. And he doesn't leave the reader in doubt as to why he did so. Having a high view of God and of the Holy Scriptures, having had some of the best training one could have had at the time of Christ's appearing, and having been raised in a home that took obedience to God as paramount, maybe even to a fault, Saul had been taught his whole life that God had chosen him and expected his obedience. If only Christians today were raised in a similar atmosphere!

Saul's Belief in a Resurrection and a Judgment

But we can add a further reason that Saul took his faith so seriously. He fervently lived his faith because of his belief in a resurrection of both the righteous and the wicked for personal judgment by God.[1] In Saul's mind there was no leeway for being lukewarm, much less indifferent or rebellious, in obeying the faith that God had revealed to the nation. He expected the Jewish people to defend their faith because they were confident that it was from God and that they would be held accountable for defending it as well as for obeying it. Not only did Saul maintain this conviction,[2] but many of the Jewish religious leaders did as well.[3] Their belief in a resurrection and in a subsequent judgment is something to consider more carefully.

Paul affirmed this belief in two places. Both times he did so while defending his faith. Luke first recorded it in Acts 23:6, quoting Saul as saying,

"I am on trial for the hope and resurrection of the dead."

While Saul is trying to be cunning in order to escape the unfair charges against him by the religious leaders, what he said is nonetheless true: he did believe in a resurrection of the dead. In fact, many of the Sanhedrin, all of them that were Pharisees apparently, believed in that resurrection just as he did. And that is a very relevant point.

Saul's belief in the resurrection of the dead and in God's judgment of all men after that resurrection was held *long before* he trusted in Jesus. But now notice that his accusers, who still

---

[1] Acts 24:14-16.

[2] Acts 23:6.

[3] Acts 23:7-9.

haven't trusted in Jesus, also believed in this resurrection and judgment as well. In God's own timing, a resurrection of both the righteous and the wicked will occur.[1] At that resurrection God will evaluate every deed that a person has performed, whether good or worthless. A recompense, or pay-back, will be meted out upon both of those kinds of actions. This Saul had believed from the time of his childhood training under Gamaliel.

Saul used these two doctrines to defend himself against the accusations of the Sanhedrin. The power of his defense is seen in the fact that the prospect that these doctrines outlined struck fear in the heart of Felix the governor.[2] Saul defended his actions, claiming not only his innocence[3] but also a good motivation for every action he had performed.[4] So without drama or pomp, Saul stated, and Luke recorded under the inspiration of the Spirit of God, that he always tried to live so that he would have no regrets when he stood before God for his own personal judgment. Saul described it this way:

> "... in view of this [a resurrection and a judgment following it], I also do my best to *maintain always a blameless conscience* both *before God* and before men." (Acts 24:16)

Now if we take this in the manner it is delivered to us in the Scriptures, namely, as a fact not to be dismissed or twisted, Saul was not only telling us what his former life and ministry were like, he was also describing his new life and calling by God. Because these doctrines guided his entire life and were not beliefs that he picked up after trusting in Jesus as God's Messiah, he was admitting to the court, and to all the world afterward, that

---

[1] Acts 24:15.

[2] Acts 24:24-25.

[3] Acts 23:1.

[4] Acts 24:16.

he had *always* lived by this standard.[1]

So, let's consider this a bit more thoroughly for just a moment. Can you imagine, even for a second, that God would reject a man whose belief in Him led him to obey the revelation that He had given and to do that extremely well? Would God reject the man who was not only zealous for Him and Him alone but even served Him professionally? Would God reject a man who lived his whole life knowing that he would give an answer to God for every decision and for every motivation behind every decision, and who experienced no conviction from God that he was out of line or had come short of what He wanted from him? This is the kind of person that Saul really was, a man in whom the one, true God was well-pleased!

But Saul isn't finished comparing his former life to his life after he trusted in Jesus. He will be very clear in affirming a vital, spiritual life before he ever trusted in Jesus. The question is, "Will we be bold enough to believe what he said as he wrote under the inspiration of the Spirit of God?"

---

[1] An even more poignant question might be, "How are you going to harmonize the fact that Saul believed in Jesus and in His all-sufficient death on the cross for his sins, yet he continued to believe that a recompense for sinning was still to be expected at each person's final judgment?" This recompense for sinning at the final judgment had been taught to him by Solomon in Eccl. 12:13-14. Apparently, Jesus' personal tutorlege of Saul had not changed this expectation in the least.

Chapter 8

Saul's Personal Testimony
Before the Gentiles

After Saul believed in Jesus as the Messiah, he denied that the new content of his faith forced him to change any of his original beliefs. So, what he is telling us is that he did not consider his previous faith incorrect; it was not misguided; it was not unspiritual; it was not inadequate in any way. *It was all that it should have been; it was all that God required of anyone.* In fact, he was exemplary in his convictions and in his manner of life.

Saul Believed the OT Scriptures

His faith had been grounded squarely upon the OT Scriptures. So, he affirmed that

> ". . . according to the Way, which they call a sect, I [do] **serve** [or I am serving] the God of our fathers, **believing everything** that is in accordance with the Law, and that is written in the Prophets; having a hope in God, **which these men cherish themselves**, that **there shall certainly be a resurrection** of both the righteous and the wicked. In view of this, I also do my best to maintain always **a blameless conscience** both **before God** and before men." (Acts 24:14-16, emphases and brackets mine)

Paul admitted the he continued his service for the same God that he had believed in before trusting Jesus, only now his service was given through a different ministry. Instead of continuing to minister as a Pharisaic teacher and as an apologetic defender of the faith God gave through the authors of the OT, he had become a preacher, a teacher, and an apostle of Jesus Christ.[1] And not only did he affirm that he was serving the same God in his new ministry as he had in his previous ministry, he also asserted that his belief system had not changed in any way. He continued to believe *all that was in accordance with the Law and that had been written in the prophets of old.*

The objective student of Scripture does not come away from this divinely inspired testimony with the *radical conversion template* that is so often used to describe Saul's new faith in Jesus. Rather, he sees a continuation of Saul's previous faith which is now more fully informed by new divine revelation. Because his previous faith was fully pleasing to God, his new faith confirmed, rather than replaced, his old faith; it further explained his old faith, but it in no way condemned it or set it aside.

Saul was Illumined, not Converted

In Saul's last defense before Festus and King Agrippa, which defense came near the end of his two-year incarceration in Caesarea, he repeated his claim that the new content of his faith and the new message that he now preached were not really new at all. That is to say, his new faith and message were not new or different from what the OT Scriptures had always taught about the coming Messiah. So, everyone should understand that when he preached, he only testified to:

> "... what the Prophets and Moses said was going to take place: that the Christ [must be connected to] suffering, and [be] the first by [reason of] His resurrection from the dead to proclaim light both to the Jewish people and to the Gentiles." (Acts 26:22-23)

---

[1] 2Tim. 1:11.

76

Saul was saying that he had already believed that the God of Israel was going to send a Messiah who would fulfill all that Moses and the prophets predicted about Him. Certainly he did not have a full understanding of all these things until Jesus explained them to him after He appeared to him on the road to Damascus. But he believed more than the average Christian does today. And the content of his faith was not altered when he trusted in Jesus as his promised Messiah.

*As a result, he was not **converted** to a different faith; he only received new revelation about his old faith.* His new faith in Jesus as Messiah reinforced his previous faith in the one, true God who had promised to send a Messiah.

> What Saul came to believe was fully consistent with what he had already believed.

Why would Saul make this declaration if what he had believed was somehow deficient? He can't be lying since this is an inspired text of Scripture and as such it can't lead us astray as, indeed, it would if it were not true. Consequently, *Saul gave us every reason to believe that if he had died **before** Jesus had appeared, his belief in and walk with the God of Israel were in every way pleasing to that God who would judge him after his death.* Jesus came to reinforce and enhance Saul's belief in the God of Israel; He did not come to start a new faith, a new religion.

Saul Was Appointed as a Minister

Lastly, when we analyze Jesus' explicit declaration concerning the reason that He appeared to Saul on the road to Damascus, what is left out shouts so loudly that it is hard to receive any longer the traditional interpretation of Saul's experience. Jesus' purpose statement for appearing to Saul is specifically stated in

Acts 26:16-18 and should be taken as a controlling idea:

> *". . . for this purpose* I have appeared to you, *to appoint you a minister and a witness* not only to the things which you have seen, but also to the things in which I will appear to you; delivering you from the Jewish people and from the Gentiles, to whom I am sending you, to open their eyes so that they may turn from darkness to light and from the dominion of Satan to God, in order that they may receive forgiveness of sins and an inheritance among those who have been sanctified by [a continuing] faith in Me." (Acts 26:16-18, emphases and bracket mine)

To come away from Saul's encounter with Jesus on the road to Damascus with any other purpose for this miraculous encounter other than the one explicitly given by God in this passage is to pervert the message God wanted all readers of Luke's inspired record to obtain. From the mouth of Jesus Himself we learn that He appeared to Saul "to appoint him a minister." Jesus didn't appear to him to *evangelize* him. He didn't appear to him to *convert* him. (Probably no more ludicrous thought can be imagined than Jesus, the incarnate Word of God, appearing to someone to convert him away from the faith God had revealed to him.) There is not a word or even so much as a hint that Jesus' purpose in appearing to Saul was to forgive all of his sins, or to impute (that is, to give or transfer) to him His perfect righteousness, or to save him from hell. These ideas, all considered orthodox concepts, must be read into the text because they are not inherently there to be read out of it.

The one purpose statement given to explain this encounter must not be missed, twisted, or enlarged upon. Jesus appeared to Saul to enlist him as His minister. Just as he had faithfully ministered for the God of Israel, now he would have the opportunity to minister for the Messiah that God had sent to Israel to fulfill the covenants and promises He had given to them through His prophets.

But since Saul was *already* a minister for God, and that *by divine calling* as we will confirm later, we might ask, "What is the difference between the ministry that he had and the one he was being given?" His new ministry would be one of witnessing **to the things that he had seen** in this encounter and **to the things that Jesus will show him** as he moved forward in his faith. Saul was basically enlisted to give his personal testimony to all who would listen to him. Saul's ministry would be much like the Gerasene demoniac's![1] Saul was being asked to share with others what the one, true God had done for him through the Messiah He had sent into the world. And as he shared his own story, his audiences' hearts would be convicted over the truth about Jesus and the supernatural, spiritual life He was offering.

As we think further about Saul's new assignment, we have to wonder about the simplicity of his calling and how it would be easy to duplicate or apply it in our lives today. Jesus is really only asking us to tell others about what He is doing in our lives. I wonder whether the reason that so few talk to others about Jesus is that Jesus isn't really doing much in their lives that they can tell others about. But if that should be true of your life, be encouraged! Jesus has a wonderful, abundant life to give to you each day. But you have to learn how to access it and live it before the world. It is a marvelous adventure. Don't stop searching until you discover what it is to be empowered by the Spirit of God. That is part of the difference between Saul's old life and ministry and the new one he found in Jesus. May you find it too.

---

[1] Mk. 5:18-20.

Section Three

What Saul Wrote About Himself

Chapter 9

Saul's Biographical Comments
in Galatians

There are two main passages in which the apostle Paul described his spiritual condition and character before he trusted in Jesus. Both of these passages are very revealing. We will look at them in chronological order, taking Gal. 1:11-17 first in this chapter and then moving to the extremely poignant passage of Phil. 3:3-9 in the following chapter. Being part of God's inspired canon of Scripture, they give us infallible testimony.

The *presumption* that has long been the dominate perspective on Saul in Christian theology is that he really couldn't have been what he claimed to be because he had not yet believed in Jesus.

Consequently, *he just thought* he was right before God when in fact he was not.

He just thought he was righteous when in fact he was self-righteous, and blind to that fact.

He just thought he had obeyed the law when such a life style is clearly impossible and therefore inadequate for his justification before God.

He just thought he was pleasing to God when in fact he was an enemy of God and hostile toward Him.

He just thought God had approved of his walk when in fact God had doomed him to hell because he had rejected Jesus.

What he thought was true of him plainly wasn't. At least that is what I had been taught.

Most people believe that Saul was a condemned man until he trusted in Jesus. And because of that *presumption*, they are naturally prejudiced against the plain statements of Scripture that seem to teach otherwise. I can fully relate to those who think this way. It was a surprise to me when I finally realized how my theological training had prejudiced me in my study of the Scriptures. I'm talking about prejudices so strong that they blinded me to what the Bible was actually trying to teach me. I couldn't hear the Scriptures until I set aside my theological grid because the Bible didn't seem to reflect, in all of its parts, the theology that was supposed to have come from it.

I finally realized that I had a decision to make: I could either hold onto my theology or believe the Scriptures. But I couldn't do both. Because I had been steeped in theology ~ and I admit that I have always loved the study of it ~ my break from it was extremely difficult.

I now know far less than I once did ~ or thought I did ~ but the Scriptures have come alive to me in a whole, new and exciting way. The message of the Bible is simpler and far easier to understand. But to say that the perspective that the Bible actually sets before its readers is different from the theological synthesis of the last five hundred years is an enormous understatement. This gap between what is considered orthodox theology and the teachings of the Bible grows the more independent my studies become. Of course, the problem could be all mine.

The Gospel Paul Preached

Unlike the systematic theologies that abound among Christians, the *gospel* that Paul preached did not originate with man. It came directly from Jesus Christ Himself just like the rest of the Scriptures themselves. Surely after being carefully instructed by Jesus Christ, he would have had an infallible plumb line to critique his own life and his former beliefs correctly.

But we *never* find one instance in which he admitted that his former beliefs were in any way inadequate or less than pleasing to God. While he does mention that he was wrong about Jesus, that admission does not nullify his previous belief in and walk with God. Neither the new instruction given to Saul by Jesus nor the convicting work of the Holy Spirit kept him from describing his pre-Christian life as blameless.[1] And since it was blameless, it was exactly what God desired.[2]

Saul's Pre-Christian Life

In his letter to the Galatians, Paul described his former manner of life. There he explained his religious convictions and lifestyle *apart from* faith in Jesus as the Messiah. He tried not only to persecute the church of God, but to destroy it.[3]

This comes as no surprise to us considering his childhood, his religious training under Gamaliel, and his zeal for God as an official Pharisee. Saul was so convinced that his Jewish faith in God and in His promises to His chosen nation, Israel, was true that any detraction from or dilution of that faith had to be dealt with severely. Saul's animosity toward the first Messianic Jews naturally leads the student to the conclusion that Saul so com-

---

[1] Phil. 3:6.

[2] Cf., Gen. 17:1 where the same term is used to describe the lifestyle God required from Abraham. Hence, one can achieve this lifestyle with or without the Mosaic Law and without Jesus.

[3] Gal. 1:13-14.

pletely believed the OT Scriptures that he wasn't going to tolerate any teaching that even gave the appearance of a rejection of his beloved, ancestral faith. And because this is so apparently true, we have to ask ourselves,

> "How can such a man be hell bound with such a commitment to walk with and honor the one, true God and His divine revelation?"

If his commitment to and zeal for God cannot be denied, and they can't be, on what grounds is Saul condemned by so many today? He is condemned based upon *the content of his faith*, or better by the lack of content in his faith. Because he had not yet believed in Jesus, it is *assumed* that he must be hell bound.

But as the members of my Thursday morning Bible study so appropriately concluded some years ago, *bad theology won't send a person to hell or keep him out of heaven*. God, the illuminator of all men, has not given the same amount of light ~ or truth, information, content (whatever you want to call it) ~ to all men. Yet He still very clearly wants to be known as *the God of all men*.[1] If we properly understand this truth, the work of Christ on the cross is not denied or even diminished; it is greatly and wonderfully expanded, being extended to all men in all ages since the time of Adam and Eve. This topic will be covered in more detail in volume four of this series, *Freedom through the Cross*.

Saul's Initial Hesitancy to Believe in Jesus

Initially Saul had a few obstacles to overcome before he could seriously entertain the idea that Jesus was God's promised Messiah. While they weren't many in number, they were major. For example, how could Jesus be the Messiah, he probably rea-

---

[1] Rom. 3:27-31.

soned, when there was no kingdom to prove His Messiahship?[1] Saul did not believe that the promised kingdom was spiritual, rather than physical, in nature as many theologians do today.

Neither Saul nor any of the other apostles would have accepted the concept of the kingdom of heaven that is generally taught today. They knew that God had promised an external, visible, earthly kingdom in the sacred Scriptures as a blessing upon David's household and for the benefit of the entire nation of Israel. And that canon of revelation was Saul's plumb line for discerning truth from error and a false prophet from a true one, as God meant it to be.[2]

Furthermore, the Messiah was supposed to rule "forever." If He ruled *forever*, He would have to live *forever*. While Jesus' resurrection had not been witnessed by Saul until his encounter with Jesus on the road to Damascus, Saul believed in a resurrection and in a divine judgment on each person afterward. What happened to Jesus' body may have been unique, but it didn't automatically make Jesus the Messiah because the Messiah, Saul was convinced, was supposed to live and reign *on the earth* forever. Those facts that Jesus died and that He had not set up the promised kingdom may have disqualified Him for consideration as the Messiah in Saul's thinking.

The commitment that Saul possessed for his "ancestral traditions" and the lengths that he was willing to go to defend them allowed him to advance in the eyes of the leaders of his Jewish faith beyond "many of his countrymen."[3] Or to put it simply: he

---

[1] Many Jews today stumble over this exact issue. They don't realize, just as Saul didn't, that the promised kingdom could be delayed because the condition for its establishment had not been met by the Jewish nation, namely, *a righteous people* walking by faith in the God who had promised them the kingdom.

[2] Cf., e.g., Deut. 13:1-4.

[3] Ibid.

demonstrated that he was "more extremely zealous"[1] about Israel's faith than they did. This was the same zeal for the same object that he had learned in his youth from Gamaliel. This was the same zeal for the same object that he maintained as he followed Jesus as an apostle. And it was the same zeal for the same object that the mob displayed when they tried to kill him in Jerusalem. This zeal pleased God because He was the object of it, regardless of the amount of content involved with it.

This description of Saul's beliefs and of his defense of those beliefs is clear and straightforward. It is a common tenet of the Christian faith that the Christian faith itself is the natural fulfillment of the Jewish faith given in the OT. *But if the Christian faith does not believe that Jesus is first and foremost the Jewish Messiah who came to fulfill God's covenants and promises to Israel, then it is not the continuation of the Jewish faith at all; it becomes a perversion and a distortion of it.*

Saul tenaciously clung to the Jewish faith that believed in the one, true God who had given inviolable promises that He had to fulfill, or He would deny His own veracity and faithfulness. If Saul was forced to make a choice between his understanding of the OT Scriptures and Jesus' claims to be the Messiah fulfilling them, he would take the Scriptures because they were certainly from God. This Jesus had to be examined in light of God's revelation.

Saul's limited, but not misguided, perspective led to his rejection of Jesus. What he needed was someone to help him better connect the dots given in the OT. When Jesus did that for him, Saul understood how Jesus could be the Messiah and yet not establish the long-awaited kingdom God had promised the na-

---

[1] Ibid.

tion. He could die but promise to return to fulfill all the unfulfilled prophecies concerning the Messiah. It was such a tiny step to take that he was finally fully persuaded that he should accept Jesus as the Messiah He claimed to be.

Saul's Consecration and Calling

In Gal. 1:15-16, Saul made an astonishing statement from our point of view today. He realized that he had been "set apart even from his mother's womb" by being born a Jew. It ought to never be denied that the Jewish people always were and still remain to be, God's chosen, *national* instrument to serve Him.

Every Jew today has the same privilege that Paul was speaking about in this verse: he had been set apart from birth to serve God uniquely by being part of a nation uniquely chosen for service.

> To be born a Jew was to have a special role in life.

His next revelation is so amazing that, if it were being reported today, we would hear a newsman say, "Stop the presses! We have a breaking story." Saul described himself not only as *set apart from the womb* but also as one who *had been called by grace*. So, "What is so news worthy about that?" someone might ask.

The poignant truth does not come out until we analyze the timing designated by the verbal tenses involved in Gal. 1:15-16. While a participle in the aorist tense can refer to contemporaneous action with that of the main verb, it is much more common for it to indicate *action preceding that of the main verb*. And in the case before us, we have two participles that are joined together by a single article producing a description of God as "the separating and calling God." Hence, these participles are attributive adjectives describing God. But they also denote instances when these attributes have been manifested. They were manifested at the time of Saul's birth and sometime in his early adult life, no one knows the exact moment, but *it was sometime before God revealed Jesus to him.*

It is undeniable that the separation that Saul described took place at birth since he adds "from his mother's womb" to help designate the time of its occurrence. The second participle, *called*, is generally related to Saul's Damascus-road experience. At that time Saul was *supposedly* saved from hell and called into apostolic service when he trusted in Jesus.

No one would argue with the suggestion that Saul was separated at birth and called into service by Jesus on the road to Damascus. Nevertheless, we must ask, "Is that really what this text is describing?" It certainly is one legitimate option. But is it the only one? Is it even the best one? Sometimes traditional answers can block other options from view. This is the case here.

There are several facts in the immediate context that mitigate against the common, theologically-driven interpretation. Verses thirteen and fourteen mention Saul's *extreme zeal* for his ancestral traditions. These traditions included a faith in the one, true God[1] and a love for Him that results in obedience [2] and even professional service.[3] These traditions require the reader to understand that Saul was

> Saul's belief in Jesus and service as His apostle simply continued the service he had been giving to God as a Pharisee.

already a believer in and follower of the one, true God *before* he

---

[1] Heb. 11:2, 6.

[2] Deut. 6:4-9.

[3] Phil. 3:5; Acts 23:6; 26:5.

believed in Jesus. Saul repeatedly said so.[1]

In addition to these things, he had been one of *the choice few* that had been raised in a strict Pharisaical home, educated under one of the greatest Rabbis of his day, and led into the professional service of God as a Pharisee. And as we take a closer look at this passage, we can discern that Saul was both *set apart* from his mother's womb and *called* **before God was pleased to reveal His Son in him**. Because both participles are governed by the same article, and because *the first participle* **must be taken** *as an antecedent action*, it would be normal to take the other participle in the same way.[2]

Consequently, God's gracious calling of Saul does not refer to his *calling to faith in Jesus*. Nor does it refer to his *calling to apostolic ministry*. It refers to his *calling to service as a Pharisee*. It was to this man, who had been formerly set apart and called to service as a strict Pharisaic Jew, that God eventually was pleased to reveal His Son.

Isn't this scenario really what we see revealed to us very clearly in Acts nine? Saul the committed Pharisee now has a revelation of Jesus presented to him after which he is enlisted as an apostle to serve Jesus. Saul's whole biography portrays a man zealous for God and totally committed to serve Him.

If he had been called to serve God as a Pharisee, he would have to be a believing follower of God (as would be, presumably, the rest of the religious leaders at the time of Christ). He couldn't be called *by God* to serve Him if he didn't believe God

---

[1] Acts 22:3-5; 23:6; 24:14-16; 26:4.

[2] An objection may be raised that these are attributive participles and not circumstantial participles and thus cannot be related to time of the main verb at all. But because Paul adds the phrase "from my mother's womb," it is merely *ad sensum* to understand these participles as describing a characteristic of God that was manifested at a time previous to His revelation of His Son in Saul.

existed. And he wouldn't have been called *by God* to give greater service as an apostle if he had been unfaithful in his previous calling because only to the one who has been faithful in small things is more given by God.[1]

Again, Saul was never Converted!

His historical, cultural background, his personal testimony approved by the Holy Spirit, and his own writings do not allow us to see a radical change in his belief system *before* he trusted in Jesus to what it was *after* he had trusted in Jesus. The traditional teaching about Saul's spiritual condition before he trusted in Jesus is such thin ice that it is a wonder that anyone ever skated out on it in the first place. Saul was not *converted*; he was *"catecheticalized."*[2] Or as I said earlier, Saul was not converted; he was illumined and blessed. He was given a lot more revelation after he trusted in Jesus ~ a little divinely administered catechetical training if you please! But that does not allow us to conclude that he was wrong about what he had believed from the OT Scriptures before trusting in Jesus. He wasn't!

There was a wonderfully smooth continuity in Saul's thinking as he became persuaded that Jesus was the fulfillment of what he had been taught by the Scriptures that he had studied from childhood. Jesus fulfilled those Scriptures; He did not change those Scriptures or nullify them in any way. He knew that the Jews were seeking eternal life (i.e., the kingdom) from them; they were, therefore, one of His best witnesses to His true identity. To isolate Jesus from His OT roots, that is, from God's purposes in sending Him, is to create a new religion around "a"

---

[1] Cf., Matt. 25:21, 23, 24-30.

[2] I made that word up but most will immediately sense how it should be taken.

Messiah cut off from the people that He came to save.[1] And that may be a more accurate description of what the Christian faith has done *to Jesus* than seeing Him as the radical game-changer that offered eternal life, that is, an abundant life, to all who continuously believe Him for it.

Because all the Biblical evidence confirms that Saul believed in, walked with, and served God prior to his faith in Jesus, it is improper to speak of Saul as being *converted*. Such terminology implies that Christianity is radically different from the Jewish faith. It is only because the Jewish faith is true that Jesus is who He is. We understand His identity correctly only by accepting what the OT, God's revelation to the Jewish people, says He is.

But we must remember that the Jewish faith had predicted the coming of the Messiah who would deliver the Jews from their enemies, establish the earthly kingdom promised to them, and bear away their sins *in a way that they had been prepared to understand*. Christianity should never have been seen as a radical break from OT Judaism. And it isn't when both faiths are properly understood.

Christianity still believes, or it ought to believe, in all of the same things that the Jew was led to believe from his sacred Scriptures. Only an unbiblical theology would lead one to veer from what was plainly written in those Scriptures. We have built a straw-man which supposedly rightly criticizes the Jewish faith portrayed for us in the OT and in the Gospels. We have failed in our analysis; the Jews have not been wrong in their OT beliefs.

---

[1] Cf., Matt. 1:21; John 1:11-12. By saving them from their sins (not from the *supposed* eternal penalty on their sins, namely, from hell), they would have the righteousness required for kingdom entrance (Matt. 5:20; 6:33; 7:21; etc.). Jesus came to establish the promised David Kingdom but because of Israel's widespread unbelief, He had to delay its establishment.

Chapter 10

Saul's Biographical Comments
in Philippians

Paul's autobiographical descriptions are quite arresting to say the least. So much is this the case that most of the time the commentaries on his statements create ways to find some presumed deficiency in them. Otherwise his statements simply can't be harmonized with the inadequate mindset that most of us have been taught to bring to the text of Scripture. But instead of rejecting what is written, we need to change the presuppositions that we bring with us to the text. Watch carefully how taking Paul's statements at face value will necessitate this change in our presuppositions and, consequently, in our theology.

When Paul described his credentials in Phil. 3:1-9, he set before his readers *facts* that were true of him. These facts and achievements separated him from most of his contemporaries. They provided him with a basis for rightful boasting. To the Philippians he described himself this way:

"Beware of the dogs, beware of the evil workers, beware of [those who promote] the mutilation [of the foreskin]; for we are the circumcision, those serving by the Spirit of God and exalting in Christ Jesus and not being confident in the flesh (even though I [am] *having confidence even in the flesh*). *If any other one supposes to be confident in the flesh, I more*: *circumcised* the eighth day, of the race of *Israel*, of the tribe of *Benjamin*, a *Hebrew* of Hebrews; according to the Law, a *Pharisee*; according to *zeal*, a persecutor of the church; *according to righteousness which is in the Law, being blameless.* But whatever things were gain to me, those I consider loss because of Christ. More than that, I count all things to be loss because of the surpassing value of *knowing Christ Jesus my Lord,* because of whom I have counted all things as loss, and I consider them rubbish in order that *I may gain Christ, and be found in Him, not having my righteousness from [coming out of or by] the Law, but that [righteousness] through the faithfulness of Christ, the righteousness of God on the basis of faith,* so that I *may know Him,* and the power of His resurrection and the fellowship of His sufferings, being conformed to His death, *if perhaps I may attain to the resurrection* from the dead." (Phil. 3:2-11, my translation, brackets, and emphases)

While so many wonderful truths could be mined from this magnificent passage, we will limit ourselves to two of them: 1.) that Saul was righteous *before* trusting in Christ and 2.) that he sought a different righteousness *after* trusting in Christ. But we must understand that *neither righteousness was any more acceptable to God than the other was.* They were different. And one was to be preferred. But they both met God's requirements in their appropriate historical and cultural contexts. In fact, it is only because God identified them both as righteous that they were so.

Righteousness from the Law

Beginning with verse six, Saul revealed, under the inspiration of the Spirit of God, that he was righteous *before* he came to faith in Jesus. He made his claim with these words:

"as to the *righteousness* which is in the Law, found *blameless.*" (Phil. 3:6, emphases mine)

Saul was claiming, with the Spirit of God's full approval, that he had successfully lived the life that God required from His chosen people. His life was just as fully approved by God as the

96

lives of Abel, Enoch, Noah, Job, and Abraham had been. And he lived this life *before* he trusted in Jesus.

Assumptions abound; most are based upon unbiblical theology. For example, it is *assumed* that the righteousness which Paul claimed for himself was a matter of self-delusion; it was a figment of his imagination. Sure, he *thought* he was righteous before God, but he really wasn't. He couldn't have been because it is *presumed* that it is impossible to be righteous before God apart from God's gift of righteousness. But we need to ask, "Is that *presumption* really taught clearly in the Bible or is it the logical deduction of man's attempt to systematize the Bible?"

The argument against the possibility that Saul could have been righteous before he trusted in Jesus is circular reasoning at best. It is a fact that Joseph, Zachariah, and Elizabeth were all righteous before God.[1] And they were declared to be so without even a hint of some imaginary gift of righteousness having been imparted to them. In fact, Zachariah and Elizabeth were declared to be righteous in the sight of God because they had . . .

> "travelled or proceeded ***blamelessly*** (the same term Saul used to describe himself) ***in all*** the commandments and requirements of the Lord." (Lk. 1:6, author's translation, notes, and emphases)

The fact is the Scriptures *explicitly* declare that Zachariah and Elizabeth were righteous because they had obeyed the Law of God blamelessly. They were not righteous because they had been given a righteousness ***to meet*** God's requirements; they were righteous because they ***had met*** God's requirements.

Like Zachariah's and Elizabeth's, Saul stated that his righteousness was a fact. What is more, he claimed that he was *blameless* in achieving the *righteousness* demanded by the Law.

---

[1] Matt. 1:19; Lk. 1:6.

We struggle with these two examples of blamelessness in righteousness because we are more guided by errant, fallible

> To gainsay what Paul said under the inspiration of the Spirit of God is to cease having the Word of God as one's authority.

theology than by God's inspired Word. What the text says is actually very straight forward. The only problem is that what it says contradicts what has been accepted as orthodox Christian teaching.

Others *assume* that Paul's righteousness was merely some form of legalism whereby he tried to gain that ever-elusive, *eternal acceptance* with God by his works (if there is such a thing revealed in the Scriptures). He wanted acceptance; he worked for acceptance; but alas, he fell short as all men must do. Isn't that what Rom. 3:23 means when it says,

> "For all have sinned and are [presently] falling short of the glory [or righteousness] of God"? (my translation and brackets)

It has been *assumed* that Saul's approach to righteousness could never put him in right standing with God. That *assumption* contradicts what Saul wrote about himself as the Spirit of God inspired the record of his past convictions. Are we going to allow bad theology to guide us in our interpretation of the Bible? Or are we going to accept the testimonies of Scripture?

Paul declared that he was righteous **before** he trusted in Jesus, and, he says, he was blamelessly so. By this inspired revelation we are *forced* to conclude that since he was *already* righteous, he was *not* in need of any other righteousness to be *imputed* to him (in the sense of being given to him as a gift apart from his deeds) in order for him to be initially accepted by God.[1]

---

[1] I am arguing *against* the accepted, theological idea that God requires a perfect righteousness in order for a person to be eternally accepted by Him. That is *not* what the

Such an idea cannot be found in any of the thirty-nine books of the OT. And if the OT is the basis for the NT, as it certainly is, it should not come as any surprise that the NT

> The idea that anyone needs an eternally secured, righteous standing for God to accept him is foreign to the Bible.

doesn't develop the idea that a *positional righteousness* is needed and must be given by God for a person to be accepted by God.

We must observe that Saul was declaring himself righteous even though he had **rejected** Jesus as the Messiah. Saul was writing these autobiographical comments almost twenty years after trusting in Jesus and having served Him throughout those years. *He never admitted to being unrighteous or of being in need of some gift of righteousness.* In fact, Saul never acknowledged any spiritual inadequacy that left him outside the circle of God's daily approval. While he did indicate the presence of spiritual struggles such as every Christian is familiar, he never left any ground to question his relationship with God because of those struggles.

Since the righteousness that Paul is talking about is one "according to the Law," it is a practical righteousness that he is describing. The Law told those to whom it was given what to think, what to feel, what to do, and how to do all those things in a way that pleased God.

> *The Law didn't tell a person what to do to go to heaven or what to do to escape hell.*

Obeying the Law was God's appointed way of practical righteousness. As a result, the Law's whole focus was upon living a life which

Bible demands; that is what man has concluded that the Bible must demand as he uses the wrong paradigm to try to understand the Bible. Paul's practical righteousness is the only righteousness that is described in the Bible. And Paul is claiming to **already** have this righteousness **before** he ever trusted in Jesus. And **that** is the point of contention.

pleased God. Righteousness for Saul was always doing the right thing, the thing that God wanted done, the way He wanted it done. God has always demanded obedience that flowed from a life of trust. Or as the Jewish Shema taught: God required everyone to love Him, but He tied loving Him to obeying His word as an evidence of that love (Deut. 6:4-9). But neither obedience to the Law nor the righteousness involved in that obedience was ever tied to going to heaven.

Is Perfect Obedience Needed for Justification?

In Rom. 2:13 the apostle Paul tells us that *it is possible* for a person to be "declared righteous," that is, "to be justified," through his obedience to the Mosaic Law. Since that belief is entirely impossible if the Reformed doctrines of total depravity and justification, involving both the forgiveness of sins and the imputation of Christ's righteousness to the believer, are true, many commentators automatically choose to see this statement as hypothetical rhetoric by Paul. In other words, they trust their theology to help them interpret this verse more than they trust the rules of hermeneutics which are non-theological. As a result, they would interpret Paul's statement something like this: if a person obeyed the Mosaic Law *perfectly*, he would be justified by God; but since he can't possibly perform that level of obedience, he can't possibly become justified by his obedience.[1]

There is no indication that Paul assumed that being justified by keeping the Law was impossible. He actually and straightforwardly affirmed its possibility: "the doer of the Law will be

---

[1] Rene A. Lopez, "Romans," The Greek New Testament Commentary (Denton, TX: Grace Evangelical Society, 2010), vol. 2, p. 633. Cf., also, Zane C. Hodges, Romans, delivered from wrath (Corinth, TX: Grace Evangelical Society, 2013), pp. 67-68.

justified." Paul was not using illocutionary rhetoric.[1] To assume that no one could fulfill the obedience necessary is to draw an unwarranted conclusion from Paul's argument. *Such a conclusion sets a Biblical-theological synthesis above Paul's inspired statement.* (Rom. 3:19-20, properly understood, do not contradict Paul's statement in Rom. 2:13 as many assume.)

In his letter to the Roman Christians, Paul was trying to establish the fact that Messianic Jews *were not* living righteously as they needed to do, just as their counter-parts, the Gentiles who knew God through His revelation to them in nature, *were not* living righteously as they needed to do. But he was not saying that they *couldn't* respond as they ought. He was only saying that they *weren't* responding as they ought. Every single person that Paul addressed or described throughout the entire book of Romans had the capacity to live a life that God could approve of. But for a variety of reasons he was not doing what he could have done. All of his addressees were falling short of God's glorious, righteous standard for living. But Zachariah and Elizabeth[2] tell us infallibly that a person can be declared righteous by keeping the Law the way God meant it to be kept, namely, by faith so that the works complete the faith exercised.[3]

Paul's statement about his fulfillment of the Law **before** his encounter with Jesus on the road to Damascus should be taken in the same way that his other affirmations in his list of "credentials" are. They all should be taken as *facts* and, as Paul intended them, as a ground for boasting. He was rightly proud of the fact that he had been an obedient Jew. The righteousness that could

---

[1] Hodges, p. 68.

[2] Lk. 1:6.

[3] Js. 2:22, 24.

be attained by obeying the law, Paul said, he attained. And what was the result of that attainment? Paul said that the result was his own *blamelessness,* a term that means the absence of guilt, blame, or fault. That is a pretty strong self-evaluation! And it was written as he was being led and directed by the Spirit of God, resulting in an inspired statement which, in the nature of the case, must be inerrant and infallible.

Richard Trench in his famous work, *Synonyms of the New Testament,* makes several very interesting comments about the term *blameless* that Paul used here. First of all, he says that it and the three other terms that he is describing "all refer to the *Christian* life and to what its character *should* be."[1] We immediately see a flaw in Trench's perspective since Paul was describing himself **before** he had become a Christian. As a result, these terms aren't restricted to *Christian* character. Rather, they must describe the *godly* character of *any* person, living at any time, as he was walking with God. Zachariah and Elizabeth,[2] a husband and wife that were both from the priestly line, and Abraham[3] were other Scriptural examples of *blameless* individuals living before the time of Christ Jesus.

Most importantly, Saul is not declaring what *should* be true or what *could* be true. He was declaring what *was* true for him just as Luke declared what was true of Zachariah and Elizabeth. They were all blameless. These are the *explicit* statements of Scripture!

Further, Trench differentiates αμεμπτος from αμομος in that

---

[1] Richard Chenevix Trench, *Synonyms of the New Testament,* "Section 103: Without Blemish, Without Spot, Faultless, Blameless, Unreprovable, Irreproachable. Baker Book House, Grand Rapids, Michigan. Copyright by Baker Book House Company, 1989, p. 401, emphases mine, however.

[2] Lk. 1:6.

[3] Gen. 17:1.

the former term, the one Paul and Luke used, supposedly means "unblamed" while the latter term means "unblemished." Not even Christ Himself, Trench says, was αμεμπτος (the term Paul used of himself!) . . .

> "since He endured the persecution of sinners who slandered Him and made false charges against Him. No matter how the saints of God may strive to be αμεμπτοι, they certainly cannot attain it, for justly or unjustly, others will find fault in them."[1]

But Trench's distinction contradicts Paul's *explicit* affirmation that he was αμεμπτος, even though he had detractors who had put him in prison. So whether or not a distinction can be discerned between αμομος, which Trench says "depicts the complete absence of fault or blemish in whatever it describes," and αμεμπτος, it is certain that Paul meant to describe himself as one without blame, fault, or guilt. He was blamelessly righteous; he was what the Law required him to be for God to justify him. And he was all of this *before* he ever trusted in Jesus.

Saul Lived at a Unique Time

While Saul's autobiographical descriptions of his spiritual life were undoubtedly true, we must remember that he was living at a transitional time in history. The God of Israel, the God that Saul had already believed in and was purposefully obeying, had recently sent the promised Messiah to Israel. The approach for living pleasingly before the Lord and the ease with which it could be carried out now changed with the resources that Jesus offered. The righteousness that Saul had attained through his obedience to the Law would not need to be attained in the same

---

[1] Trench, p. 402.

way going forward.[1] In Jesus, God made available new revelation and blessings. These may now be received and used for the attainment *and experience* of the practical righteousness God required. There is no positional or forensic righteousness described in the Scriptures.

Saul is clearly the personification of the transition from the old economy of the Mosaic Law to the new economy of Messianic Life (i.e., eternal life). He illustrates how someone living prior to the time of Jesus' actual four-year ministry could meet God's standard and live a life pleasing to Him. And after believing in Jesus and receiving the blessings that He was offering, he met God's standard for living righteously in the new economy.

Saul trusted God as he responded to the Law God had given him to follow. And God justified Saul's lifestyle, reckoning his faith responses for the righteousness that He required. Upon trusting in Jesus, Saul was given the Holy Spirit and access to a new life. By the use of these resources through faith, Saul could manifest a righteousness in his response rather than have it only *attributed* to him because of the faith he had exercised in his response. In other words, his response now would actually *be* righteous because he would partake of Jesus Christ's own righteous life for his act of obedience. While God justified both responses, only his latter one was performed *from* a righteous life. So, in Saul we see two kinds of righteousness, both fully pleasing to God.

---

[1] The function of these resources and the experience of them is twice referred to as a salvation (Mk. 16:15-16; John 10:9, 27-28). But neither reference refers to a person's initial faith in Jesus. That ought to help clarify the misuse of the concept of being saved in Christian jargon today. While the resources themselves are received at a point in time one-for-all, their experience is an on-going phenomenon.

Confidence in the Flesh

Saul's fulfillment of the righteous demands of the Law and his resulting blamelessness was part of his "confidence in the flesh." Judging by all of the credentials that Saul lists, having confidence in the flesh arose from several venues. What he was and what he had by birth was one source for his boasting. Another was being raised in a God-fearing home. And still another was the zeal that he possessed for his personal faith. That zeal was manifested in his righteously obedient lifestyle.

His testimony here is quite transparent if our vision is not clouded by the fogs of inadequate theology. *Saul was what God desired all men to be from the*

> Saul's righteousness was attained by his natural abilities and capacities as he walked by faith.

time of Moses until the time of Christ. And with the new resources that he received when he believed in Jesus, he would become what God desires all men to be from the time of Christ's ascension until His return to earth. The two kinds of righteousness of which Saul spoke were equally acceptable to God even though they were not qualitatively the same nor were they achieved in the same manner.

Righteousness from Faith in Jesus

While Saul was rightly proud of the righteousness that God had declared over his life in the flesh, yet that righteousness paled before the brilliance of the righteousness found in Christ Jesus. As a result, Paul's new, life-long goal was being found in Jesus,[1]

---

[1] Being in the subjunctive mood, Paul's statement denotes a goal that was possible to attain but not certain of its fulfillment.

not having my righteousness which [is] of the Law, but rather the one [a righteousness which is] through the faithfulness of Christ,[1] the righteousness [which comes] from God upon [my] faith . . ." (Phil. 3:9, author's translation, brackets, and emphases)

The righteousness that Paul sought was not like the one Saul had formerly attained *through the flesh,* that is, by his own innate abilities as he walked in faith. There was nothing wrong with his former righteousness; it was exactly what God required up until the time that He sent His Son into the world. But now that Jesus has come, a different righteousness is possible. This righteousness is what a person actually is (or becomes at each moment) in the process of performing God's will. With this righteousness the condition for the kingdom's establishment will surely be met. If a person continues to live the old way, God's standard is being met even though the quality of the obedience produced is, in a sense, *uninspired.* But that does not mean that he would necessarily be living "in sin." It only means, among other things of course, that many blessings will be missed, and life will be harder to live as God is pursued.

An illustration may help. My daughter teaches language arts for seventh graders. On some writing assignments she gives full credit for doing the essay or poem that has been assigned irrespective of the quality of the content that is written. So, if the student analyzed the subject correctly, gave the required number of proofs, with accurate citations and references, and identified or used the required figures of speech, an A would be given to that student for doing all that was asked.

On the other hand, the students, who poured their hearts into the essay or poem and seemed to be *inspired* in what they

---

[1] Cf., Rom. 3:22 for this same prepositional phrase.

wrote, would get a grade of 100% on the assignment. While both grades are A's, the latter one is qualitatively superior to the former one. The latter one simply stood out as anyone who compared them could see. Being *inspired* even made the task easier to accomplish.

The Law was given to Israel *after* they had been experiencing a relationship from faith with the one, true God. Hence, it was *never* a means of salvation or of justification, as those terms are generally understood today (but **not** as this book is presenting them! And I hope you have discerned that vast difference). The Law was given to define the way of life, or lifestyle, that God desired His chosen people to live. And if they would live by His Law, He would **justify** their lifestyle, that is, He would declare it to be righteous. And then in time, He would send His Messiah to bring about their **salvation** from all of their enemies because they would've met His condition of living righteously.

Paul was more than excited about leaving behind *the righteousness that he had achieved as he followed the Law in relationship with his God*. This "obedience in relationship" was set forth as the only means of receiving God's declaration of righteousness in the pre-Christ era. But now God has established a new approach to righteousness. Paul said that he would rather use the new approach than continue living under the Law and working for the old righteousness. One was done tiresomely *in the flesh*[1] (that is, by one's own *natural abilities* responding to God in faith) while the other was done by the power of the Spirit.[2] That is just one major difference between them.

---

[1] Cf., Acts 15:10-11. The use of flesh here is not the same as Paul uses in Rom. 6-8. There it is a negative source for our responses. Here it is a positive source similar to Matt. 22:37. Contrary to the doctrine of total depravity, man's constitution is not totally sinful.

[2] Cf., Rom. 8:4-6.

In the old way, a person had to obey God as he trusted Him with the situation and its consequences. James explained how this worked when he said,

"Was not Abraham our father *justified by works* when he offered up Isaac his son on the altar?" (Js. 2:21, emphasis mine)

The question that James asked expected his readers to answer in the affirmative: *Yes! Abraham was justified by works* when he offered up Isaac his son on the altar. The passage in Gen. 22:1-18 is simple and clear. God told Abraham what He wanted him to do.[1] Abraham obeyed,[2] trusting God[3] with the situation and the consequences of his actions.[4]

We know that what Abraham did he did in faith[5] and that it was his faith and not his obedience alone that God justified.[6] God cannot justify works without faith, neither does He *usually* justify faith without works.[7] The only time He does justify faith without works is when He commands a person to do nothing but believe.[8] But most of God's commands involve giving a response of some kind or performing some deed as the person trusts in Him as Abraham did when he offered Isaac on the altar. Both James and Hebrews tell us that a working faith is a pleasing faith (Js. 2:14-20; Heb. 11).

---

[1] Gen. 22:1-2.

[2] Gen. 22:3-4.

[3] Gen. 22:5. Note that he says, "*I and the lad* will go yonder; and *we will ... return to you.*"

[4] Heb. 11:17-19. Because Isaac was the seed of promise through whom God had promised to give Abraham a multitudinous off-spring, Abraham believed that God would raise Isaac from the dead if he had to kill him on the altar.

[5] Js. 2:22.

[6] Js. 2:23-24.

[7] Js. 2:14-20.

[8] Cf., Gen. 15:5-6; Ex. 14:13-14.

It should not go unnoticed that *justification is pronounced **after the works are done*** (cf., e.g., Ps. 106:30-31). And it is only in the declaration or pronouncement of righteousness that we know that the response pleased God. But with the new righteousness the process is a little different.

In the righteousness that is found in Jesus, it is *an experience* of righteousness as well as *a declaration* of it. God the Father justifies the one who is "of faith in Jesus." Because justification has been misunderstood as a once-for-all event in which God declares a person to be in right standing before Him due to his faith in Jesus His Son, Rom. 3:26 has been naturally misunderstood also. Logically, if justification is a one-time event, and if it takes place on the condition that faith is placed in Jesus, then the faith that gains this justification is a simple, single expression of trust as well. But both in the prequel and in this book so far, it has been established that justification is not a one-time event, then neither is the faith in Jesus that obtains it.

The faith that Paul had in mind when he wrote Rom. 3:26, he described in Gal. 2:20 when he said,

> "I have been crucified with Christ; and I not longer live, but Christ lives in me; and **that which [i.e., the life that] I now live in the flesh, I live by faith in the Son of God** who loved me and [so] gave Himself over for me." (clarifying brackets and emphases mine)

Paul was referring to faith as a continuous trust, reliance, or dependence upon God, one that sustains a spiritual fellowship with God and experiences the life of Jesus within. His references to faith in both Rom. 3:26 and Gal. 2:20 are not once-for-all or one-time responses of faith. He is describing a faith that trusts in Jesus to live through a person in such a way that he

> The faith described in Rom. 3:26 takes care of the frailty described in Rom. 3:23.

109

no longer "falls short" of what God is requiring from him. This daily trust in Jesus, which is a moment by moment reliance upon the Holy Spirit, produces the spiritual triumph the Bible describes as justification. Thus, it is a continuous trust in Jesus to produce a righteous life within so that it can be manifested in the responses we give to every stimulus we receive.

In the old way, *practice* was the focus.[1] In the new way, a *presentation* is the focus.[2] In the old way, the burden was upon the believer even though he walked by faith in God as Abraham did. In the new way, the burden is upon the Holy Spirit to whom we must present our members for His employment or use. In the old way, the power, wisdom, and virtue arose from within the person as he was responding to God and His revelation. In the new way, the power, wisdom, and virtue is infused within the believer by the Holy Spirit who takes from Christ Jesus what He has promised to give to His dependent follower and fills the trusting believer with it.

When Paul left behind *the way of righteousness through the Law*, and sought *the way of righteousness upon faith in Jesus*, he was choosing Spirit-empowered living **by** faith over self-empowered[3] living **with** faith. The latter meets the righteous standard of God by the faith that is expressed; the former by-passes man's human abilities entirely, allowing Christ's righteous life to be manifested apart from man's limitations. In both approaches, the blood of Christ has to be applied to the person for God to be able to declare the responses that are given righteous.[4]

---

[1] E.g., Gal. 3:12.

[2] Rom. 6:12-13.

[3] This is not a reference to the "self" of indwelling sin, but to the innate, inherent abilities of each human which are to be used in loving God in fulfillment of God's commands..

[4] Rom. 3:24-25; 1John 1:7.

The second approach to righteousness is better than the first in the same way that the New Covenant is better than the Mosaic Law. They both have the will of God as their goal. But the New Covenant will accomplish it from a new heart within while the other one needed a sacrificial system to help accomplish it. Both covenants involve works; but the New Covenant provides a new heart to perform those works while the Mosaic Covenant had to depend upon man's limited resources for the obedience to be given.

Is it not plain that both of these kinds of righteousness are performed by a person who is in relationship with God? Is it not obvious that the former righteousness requires us to see Saul as an acceptable person in the sight of God? God said he was righteous and that blamelessly. Those propositions can be denied or minimized only when the Bible is no longer one's guide.

Section Four

What Saul Leads us to Believe

Chapter 11

Distinguishing Acceptance, Justification, and Salvation

In this chapter I will try to explain some of the ramifications of what we should have learned from Saul's transition from having a walk that was approved by God to being (Biblically) saved by Jesus and being (Biblically) justified by the Father. Of course, we have to limit our discussion. But everything suggested in this chapter is demanded from the truths we've learned from Saul's spiritual condition, both before he trusted in Jesus and after he had received Him as his Messiah.

Acceptance by God

The term *acceptance* is the word I chose in the second draft of my book, *The Prodigal Paradigm*, to represent the result of a person's *supposed* initial faith in God or his initial faith in Jesus. I say *supposed* initial faith in God since there is no record of one given in the entire OT Scriptures. Not one. So when the NT opens up, and we observe individuals placing an initial faith in Jesus, it is a mistake to assume that their initial faith in Jesus was their initial faith in the God of the Bible.

> *Belief in Jesus in the Gospels is actually the continuation of a previous faith in God.*

Why is this such an important observation to make? It is important because it proves that justification does not occur at initial faith as our theological systems tell us that is does. As in the case of Abraham in the OT, those who are *justified* by God for their faith in Jesus are being commended for their *spiritual walk*.

If justification is related to the Christian's walk, then redemption, reconciliation, ransom, and propitiation, because they are, according to Reformed theology, *assumed* to take place with justification, must also relate to the Christian's walk as well. That possibility throws our historical, theological understanding into a tizzy. In fact the case is actually worse than that.

As they now stand, our theological positions on justification and its accompanying doctrines are no longer possible. We have been mistaken, and we must now correct that mistake or lose all credibility.

After I discovered that the term justification was not used in the Scriptures for man's initial faith in God, I *assumed* that I only needed a new term to designate man's initial faith and all the blessings that are *supposed* to be given at that point. But it occurred to a friend of mine who was reading the manuscript of *The Prodigal Paradigm* that I was trying to name and describe a phantom, a ghost that no one had ever seen. I was *assuming* that the Bible actually made a big deal out of the point of initial faith (as my friend and I had been taught in seminary). He suggested that maybe I was actually passing on to others a tradition that is nothing more than *an unproven and unprovable assumption.*

His suggestion hit me like a ton of bricks. I almost instantly knew he was correct. I had already observed in the manuscript that he was reading that the Bible *never* mentions

> All the theological baggage that is dumped at the scene of initial faith is pure conjecture.

initial faith in the thirty-nine books of the OT. Consequently, it is

116

impossible for anyone to know what was taking place there. In fact, it is impossible to be sure that such a point even exists!

Before my friend shared his observation on initial faith with me, I had concluded that, since the Bible *never* mentions or describes a person's initial faith in God, the presumed event must not be all that important. If it were, the Bible would surely address it, right?

My conclusion was a safe one. My friend's suggestion was a little more radical. And he was surely correct in his analysis: I was passing on to others teachings that the Bible never condoned. It is past time that the theological baggage of unfounded *assumptions* and pure *conjectures* be lost in transit instead of being passed on to the next generation. There is no need to come up with an appropriate name for a person's initial faith. Nothing happens there of any consequence. If it did, the Bible would surely tell us, and it would tell us quite plainly.

The ramifications of this testable fact are enormous. It not only demands that our theology change, it also requires a new perspective in how we view all people and how we address them in our evangelistic presentations. In evangelism we ought to be telling people the "good news about Jesus Christ." But that good news concerns living life now; it does not concern our eternal destiny. Let it suffice to suggest for the present that our message is fabricated from the construction materials of a poorly formulated systematic theology

Justification

Justification does not refer to the divine activities that are *presumed* to take place when a person, *supposedly*, initially trusts in God in the OT. And since the apostle Paul uses Abraham's justification to explain everyone else's justification,[1] the NT doesn't give us any latitude to expand upon its concept. Actually, justification has nothing to do with forgiveness of past sins or with the *supposed* imputation (the grant of a righteousness that is not inherent in a person's present situation) of Christ's righteousness to the one expressing faith.

In justification God declares that a person and/or his response on a particular occasion is a righteous one because he gave it in faith as he was attempting to carry out the revealed will of God. It is the responsive person's trust in God, and that alone, as it was in Abram's case, that is reckoned, or accounted, or taken by God *for* righteousness.

God is giving, accounting, or crediting, and, in that sense alone, imputing righteousness *conditionally*. He is accounting it to a person's credit whenever he and/or his response meets His expectations or standard. Never in all of the Scriptures is Christ's personal righteousness reckoned upon a person in the fashion suggested by many of our present-day theologies.[2]

When God justifies an individual, He declares that his present response meets with His approval because it was performed in faith. In other words, this person's present response, due to *the manner in which it was performed*, obtains God's commendation. This commendation is similar to the one that God will give to the true disciple at the end of his life. After the true disciple has demonstrated consistent faithfulness, he will hear, "Well done, good and faithful servant!" That is the declaration

---

[1] Rom. 4:22-25.

[2] Neither 1Cor. 1:30 nor 2Cor. 5:21 will be able to save this doctrine since the context of both verses is about walking with God and not about coming to God in initial faith. The proper parallel to 2Cor. 5:21 and Christ's being made sin is Rom. 8:3-4. 1Pet. 2:24-25 is explanation of being or becoming the righteousness of God in Christ at that moment..

that God is proclaiming inaudibly today over each response of faith that a person gives. That, and that alone, is the Biblical doctrine of justification.

Justification does not describe a courtroom scene; it describes a living room scene in which the heavenly Father commends an obedient response by His son. Hence, the scene is not about guilt or pardon; it is about accountability and praise. *The Father is simply evaluating what His son has done.* Pure and simple.

Each faith response meets God's approval because it depended upon God's intervention in his life to use the obedience He was requiring. The actual good works that are performed, then, are only the vehicles that carry the freight that God wants delivered in the circumstance, namely, a trust in Him to intervene (in the OT) or a trust in Jesus to give eternal life every time it is needed (in the NT). So, if the good work does not carry the correct payload, namely, *faith*, God can't justify the act.

> God is not looking for flawless obedience; He is looking for faith.

To illustrate I would explain that when God commands His children today to love, He isn't looking for the best love that His sons and daughters can produce; He is looking for the divine love that His Spirit can produce in and through us. This love is only manifested as a person walks by faith, trusting the Spirit of God to produce the love that is needed and with that love the power and wisdom to implement it. [1]

That is the response that God sets His commendation upon.

That is the response that He justifies.

That is a righteous response by God's standard.

That ought to be a great relief to all the perfectionists living

---

[1] Gal. 5:16-23, 25.

among us! And, of course, this illustration only describes those who have heard the message about Jesus and have received Him. This is not the standard that God held His people to in the OT. Nor is He holding people to it today if they have never heard of Jesus and the divine resources that He is offering. God only holds them accountable to live by faith using their own innate abilities that were referred to earlier.[1]

Salvation

As we have just seen, justification is all about works! In fact, without works there can be no justification, typically speaking. According to the old paradigm of Reformed theology, that means that justification and salvation cannot be the same thing. Salvation has almost universally been described as God's guarantee of a deliverance from hell accompanied by a promise of heaven without the involvement of any works at all. But upon closely investigation, it may be true that both justification and salvation involve works. That hypothesis is sure to create a lot of spiritual heart burn for many Christian.

It has been almost the universal understanding of Paul's letter to the Ephesians that the *salvation* to which Paul referred did not involve works. That has been my own opinion as well until this final draft of this book. But as I looked more closely at what Paul told the Ephesians (2:9) and as James' comments in his letter to dispersed Messianic Jews (2:21-24) kept ringing in my ears, I have been forced to change my view. To the Ephesians, Paul said,

"For by grace you have been saved through faith; and that [salva-

---

[1] E.g., Matt. 22:37; Rom. 6:12-13; etc.

120

tion is] not of yourselves, it is the gift of God; *not as a result of works*, that no one should boast." (Eph. 2:8-9, emphasis mine)

The salvation to which Paul referred was not *by* works, nor did it **guarantee** good works as necessary **results**. But it was not **apart from** good works either (as was the justification that Paul mentioned in Rom. 3:28[1]). We must not *assume,* as I have until very recently, that the term Paul used in Eph. 2:9 has the same meaning as the term he used in Rom. 3:28. Something may not arise *from* (εκ) good works while at the same time it may still be accompanied by good works. In fact, by including faith in the conditions for the salvation that he mentioned, Paul wanted us to understand that works were involved (just as James told his readers that works complete faith), but they were not the cause or source of the salvation in question. God's grace was the cause, but *His grace worked through the good works of faith.*[2]

That works are typically involved in *justification* is clearly stated by James, the half-brother to our Lord, when he writes upon this subject in a context on *vibrant faith.* Interestingly enough, the idea of *being saved* is also relate to the same circumstances or argument that James was describing. He explained to his readers the place of works in justification when he said,

> *Salvation from sins leads to the performance of good works whereas justification is God's evaluation of the good works that have been performed.*

"Was not Abraham our father *justified by works,* when he offered up Isaac his son on the altar? . . . You see that a man *is justified by works,* and *not by faith alone.*" (Js. 2:21, 24, emphasis mine)

---

[1] The good works that Paul was forbidding in Romans were limited to *works of the Law of Moses.* Justification typically involves works. Paul's argument in Romans was to show that *the works of the Law of Moses* did not need to be followed for a person to be *righteous.*

[2] Cf., Gal. 5:6. Note the concept of faith working through the love that is shown to others.

James was saying that works are the "completion" of faith; they are the inevitable manifestation of a *living* or *vital* faith. But faith may not be either living or vital; it may be idle or dead instead. And a dead faith is still a real faith; an idle faith is still genuine. But when it is either idle or dead, it is unfruitful. To conclude that an unfruitful faith is fake is a *non-sequitur*. While it is common to hear such proclamations concerning faith, those proclamations are based upon poor theology rather than good exegesis.

The salvation that James mentioned described a deliverance from the temptation to show partiality to the rich while withholding alms to those in need within a church congregation. Each time a member was *saved* from succumbing to such temptations, God *justified* those responses, calling them righteous.

Paul broached the same message when he designated the means of salvation in a letter to Titus, saying,

> "… He **saved** us, **not on the basis of deeds** which we have done *in righteousness*, but **according to His mercy**, by the washing of regeneration and renewing by the Holy Spirit, whom He poured out upon us richly through Jesus Christ our Savior, that **being justified by His grace** we might be made heirs according to the hope of eternal life." (Tit. 3:5-7, emphases mine)

> *Salvation from sins leads to the performance of good works whereas justification is God's evaluation of the good works that have been performed.*

Notice that the salvation here is not from hell but from a wicked lifestyle as it is in the letter of James. God's mercy and grace are certainly involved. But, while salvation does not **result from** (εκ) works,[1] it is *not necessarily without good works either*.[1] The exclu-

---

[1] Tit. 3:5; Eph. 2:8-9.

sion of good works from the salvation mentioned in Tit. 3:5 and Eph. 2:8-9 either overlooks the *explicit* mention of good works by Paul to Titus or the nature and function of faith (Js. 2:22, 24).

We ought to notice that Paul could speak of "being justified by God's grace" in Tit. 3:7 since God accounts or credits, and in that sense, reckons the believer's faith *for* the righteousness that is required to meet His divine standard. Hence, it is not the quality of the person's actual performance that God is taking into account. It is his dependence; it is his faith.

The immature, new believer does not have to give a mature response for that response to be approved by God. He just needs to be trusting God to supply to him everything that he needs to give the response that God wants him to give. He should be also trusting God to use the response that he is giving to positively impact the person to whom the response is being given.

Similarly, the naïve believer does not have to give a wise, discerning response for God to reckon his response as meeting His standard of righteousness. But, once again, he does need to trust God to supply to him all that he does not have in order to give the response that God is requiring from him and, then, to use the response he gives to accomplish results that are beyond any man's ability to achieve himself.

> A man can be *justified* by God *without* believing in Jesus. But Jesus never offers a salvation from hell by grace alone.

It is faith that God looks for in every response. Because that is true, the believer is freed up to be himself and to respond at the

---

[1] Notice Tit. 3:5 mentions "works or deeds done in righteousness" and Phil. 2:12-13 talk about working out one's salvation, that is, working for the present experience of the salvation that Jesus is offering. In all three passages (Tit. 3:5, Eph. 2:8-9, and Phil. 2:12-13) the salvation is from personal sins (namely, a wicked lifestyle).

spiritual level that he has achieved rather than pretending to be something or someone that he is not.

The concept of salvation is very broad, including within its scope at least five different kinds of "rescues or deliverances." Depending upon the context alone, the spiritual salvation that may be emphasized by a writer of Scripture may be one of the following five rescues or deliverances:[1] 1.) saved from the personal sins that are committed;[2] 2.) saved from this present evil age;[3] 3.) saved from the domination of indwelling sin (or the body of sin or the flesh), by receiving the Holy Spirit who infuses eternal life into the one believing;[4] 4.) saved from the experience of the Great Tribulation that is coming upon the earth to purify its inhabitants;[5] and 5.) delivered (saved!) *from* the hand of all who hate you and *into* the promised Messianic Kingdom.[6] Each one deals with life on earth, not the afterlife.

From this list, it ought to be obvious that salvation is not the same thing as justification. Salvation, regardless of which of the five aspects is under discussion, describes *how God worked* in a person's life to deliver him from various dilemmas. Justification, on the other hand, is God's evaluative declaration upon *man's response* to some situation that had confronted him. In salvation, what God has done is the focus. In justification, what man has done is the focus. In salvation, God is always saving man from

---

[1] These are not meant to cover all the rescues that could be mentioned, but only those that have the term σωζω (or one of its cognates) clearly related to it in a given context and are spiritual in nature. Consequently, daily, physical salvations, healings and exorcisms are not included here.

[2] Matt. 1:21; Lk. 7:36-50; Eph. 2:1-10.

[3] Acts 2:40, 47; Gal. 1:4.

[4] Mk. 16:15-16; John 16:12-15; Gal. 5:16-17; Eph. 3:16-17. Cf., John 10:9, 27-28 as well.

[5] 1Thess. 5:9-10; Dan. 9:24-25; Rev. 3:10.

[6] Rom. 10:1-15; 11:14, 25-27; Matt. 19:23-25; 24:13-14.

something. In justification, God is always declaring that man has given righteous responses in the situations that he had to face. *In justification, man relies upon God. In salvation, God saves the man who is relying upon him.*

The Example of Cornelius

Hopefully this last example will convince the reader that salvation is not the same thing as justification or some *supposed* initial and permanent acceptance with God. This example of the distinction between justification and salvation is given in the Book of Acts, chapters ten and eleven, in the story of the centurion by the name of Cornelius. This man was *already pleasing to God*, and his deeds, done in devotion to the faith he had accepted from the Jews, found approval (*were justified*) with God,[1] his servants, his soldiers, and his Jewish friends.[2] Yet, he still needed to be taught about the future salvation of Messiah and to be given the resources that would enable him to gain that salvation when Jesus finally sets it up.

Not too many years ago, I was teaching through the Book of Acts and came to story about Cornelius in Acts ten. I thought I'd get out a commentary that I trusted and see how it dealt with the description of Cornelius, given by Luke the historian in verses one through four. That passage portrays Cornelius in rather glowing terms. There is no indication that Luke was not being his usual, factual self as he penned this part of his account. His historical narrative declared,

> "Now there was a certain man at Caesarea named Cornelius, a centurion of what was called the Italian cohort, a **devout** man, and

---

1 Cf., Acts 10:1-4; Heb. 11:2;
2 Cf., Acts 10:22.

one who *feared God* with all his household, and *gave many alms to the (Jewish) people*, and *prayed to God continually*. About the ninth hour of the day he clearly saw in a vision an angel of God who had just come in to him, and said to him, 'Cornelius!' And fixing his gaze upon him and being much alarmed, he said, 'What is it, Lord?' And he said to him, *'Your prayers and alms have ascended as [for] a memorial before God.'*" (emphases mine)

Here we have set before us a spiritually *devoted* man, and one who *feared God*, and led his whole household to the same place spiritually. He was also a generous man as well as *a man who prayed continually to God.*[1] Importantly, his God was the one, true God of the Jewish people.

When I read that description, I thought, "My goodness! If he was not a man of faith in God, what was he? If Jesus had not come in his lifetime, would I not consider him a man who had lived a life pleasing to God?" I answered that question in my mind affirmatively, "Yes, I think I would."

Since Cornelius did not learn the things that he needed to know to be saved (at some undisclosed point in the future) until *after* Peter preached to him, I found myself confused a bit. He certainly seemed to be described as a man with whom God was pleased because He responded directly to him by sending an angel to direct him to Peter for additional revelation. But in light of so many commentaries that find some inadequacy or deficiency in Luke's wording, I was torn.

He gave every appearance of being a person who believed in God and who was fully in step with God, yet by God's own evaluation of him, he still lacked information that he needed in order to be saved.

---

1 Note that God heard his prayer (Acts 10:4), and yet, according to John 9:31, God does not hear "sinners" when they pray. Notice also that the second half of John 9:31 is almost an exact description of Peter's portrayal of Cornelius (Acts 10:35)!

What was I missing?

How do I fit all of the facts together?

> How do I connect the dots without diminishing or discounting some of the elements spelled out for me in the passage?

The system of thinking that I had been taught could provide no answer. That system had mistakenly equated the supposedly needed initial acceptance by God with both justification and salvation. These all are supposed to occur at the same moment, or so I had been taught.

The commentary, that I retrieved from my library, instead of consulting and propounding an accepted theological view of the passage, an approach some rightly call consensus theology today, said,

> "Many people have, I think, mistaken Cornelius' condition. There can be no question that he was *already a regenerated man*; that is, *born again*."[1] (emphases mine)

"Whoa!" I thought, finding myself both comforted and confused. I was comforted because this commentator was allowing the clear description of Cornelius' spiritual condition to stand as evidence of his acceptability before God. He didn't try to redefine the terms or explain away the description Luke gave.

He didn't try to say that he was *devout* but somehow that devotion was lacking some unspecified element, making it unworthy of a genuine believer. He didn't try to convince his readers that Cornelius' *fear of God* was somehow less than God de-

---

[1] H. A. Ironside, *Lectures on the Book of Acts*, Loizeaux Brothers, New Jersey, 1943, p. 245. While I agree with Ironside that Cornelius was accepted by God, he was not a regenerated man; he was not born again. That comes only through faith in Jesus as John 1:11-13 and John 3:3, 5 clearly teach. Regeneration is the reception of eternal life in my opinion.

sired from man when He commanded man to fear Him.[1] And he didn't try to minimize Cornelius' *generosity* or his *prayer life*. His generosity was not manipulative nor did his prayer life fail to commune with God. Since this is a rather old commentary, I received additional encouragement: objectivity still lives!

So, I was greatly comforted that Ironside took Luke's description seriously instead of trying to explain it away because it didn't fit into the accepted theologies of his day or ours. And I was further comforted because I intuitively knew that Luke's description of Cornelius couldn't be that of a person who was lost and eternally condemned to hell. I knew he had not believed in Jesus yet, but it seemed too obvious to me that character like that had to flow from a divine relationship.

Once I began to see a distinction between *justification* and *salvation*, and had rejected the notion of an *initial acceptance* with God because it is not discussed in the Bible, the episode of Cornelius and Peter made perfect sense. And it did so without having to reject or redefine the description of Cornelius that Luke gave his readers.

He had developed an impressive faith in the one, true God through the agency of some of the religious leaders or laypersons in Israel in the first century. (And if they could teach a person how to walk with Yahweh, what would we naturally expect their spiritual state to be?) He reverently feared God. This fear led to both his service to Israel as well as to his own personal prayer life. It drew him to the God about whom he was learning just as Moses said it ought to do.[2]

Jesus consistently explained that God normally gives more

---

[1] E.g., Ex. 20:18-20; Prov. 1:7.
[2] Cf., Ex. 20:18-20.

information to the person who is responding to the light that he has.[1] That is what happened to Cornelius. That is both the lesson we must learn here and the example that we must follow in our own lives. When we stop learning, we stop growing spiritually.

When Peter got to Cornelius' house, he preached Jesus just like Philip had done with the Ethiopian eunuch.[2] When Cornelius and his household believed in Jesus, they understood *how the salvation that Jesus offered could be obtained*. They were also indwelt by the Holy Spirit and baptized. And from other Scriptures we know that at that same moment of faith they received eternal life.[3]

By maintaining the distinction between a spiritual walk that God justifies and the salvation that is eventually obtained as a result of a justified life lived to God's glory (and in this case through a justified life lived by faith in Jesus), the text of Acts ten and eleven can be taken literally and straightforwardly. If the distinction is not maintained, a series of *conjectures* must be formulated about Cornelius' spiritual state before Peter ever preached to him[4] about the lesson Peter learned from this experience,[5] and about the meaning of the term saved.[6] None of these conjectures are likely to fulfill the requirements of the other Scriptures that must be harmonized with this one.

All of the OT saints, all those addressed by Jesus in the Gospels, the Ethiopian eunuch, Saul, and Cornelius demonstrate for

---

[1] E.g., Lk. 12:48; Matt. 13:10-12; John 7:17; 14:21, 23.

[2] Acts 8:26-39.

[3] John 6:47.

[4] Acts 10:1-4.

[5] Acts 10:34-35.

[6] Acts 11:14-18. Salvation here is primarily *the deliverance into* the coming kingdom of Messiah, make possible by walking according to the Holy Spirit with the "life" (i.e., eternal life) that He can repeatedly infuse as needed within the believing person.

us that one can believe in God and live a life pleasing to Him *before* he knows about or trusts in God's Messiah. Salvation, on the other hand, describes the deliverance promised by the hand of the Messiah. Jesus offered the Holy Spirit and eternal life to enable the believers to qualify for the obtainment of that salvation or entrance into Messiah's future kingdom.

Jesus did not change what God was already doing; He offered additional resources to maintain a spiritual walk that represents God to the world around. Since the standard for that spiritual walk has gotten higher in the NT and since the spiritual warfare in the world in which the spiritual walk must be carried out, is more intense, God provides in His Messiah the resources to meet God's new standard and to stand firm against all the Devil's schemes and attacks. But the overall plan doesn't change in the least: *God created all men to represent Him as they walk in fellowship with Him and rule over the earth.* How well they carried out their stewardships will be the subject of their judgment in the afterlife.

Chapter 12

Diagraming the Teaching of the Bible

Sometimes it is a lot easier to follow what someone else is saying if he diagrams it schematically. I will attempt to illustrate what is most often being said today with what this book is suggesting. By now you ought to realize that this is far from an academic exercise. The ramifications of this new paradigm impacts how we see all the people in the world, how we approach them with the message of Jesus, how we think about our walk with God, how we understand God's plan for the whole earth, how each person is commissioned by God and remains responsible to Him for how he lives his life, and many, many more issues besides.

Justification	Sanctification	Glorification
X_(_____	_____X_____	_____)_X
• Initial Faith	• Continuing Faith	• The End of Faith
• Birth	• Growth	• Translation into
• Redemption	• Walk with God	Heaven
• Reconciliation		
• Ransom, Propitiation, Salvation		

Almost the entirety of Christendom believes that there is a point of initial faith for a person. At that point of initial faith lots of things *supposedly* happen that are all great blessings to the new believer. Some of these are as follows:

1. He is forgiven of all of his sins, past, present, and future[1]
2. He is declared permanently righteous before God[2]
3. He is saved for heaven & from hell[3]
4. All other major salvific terms fit at this initial point of faith as well. These include redemption, reconciliation, ransom, propitiation, and salvation. All occur at the point of initial faith, securing a future destiny in heaven for all eternity.

On the graph the initial response of faith is called justification, and it is at this point that God declares a person in right standing before Him, a point that can never be *repeated again*. God's declaration of righteousness or of right standing before Him is based upon faith alone apart from any works. It is supposed to be a matter of God's grace and not dependent upon man's works, at least not *initially*.[4] At the same moment that justification occurs, it has been supposed that redemption, reconciliation, ransom, propitiation, and salvation also take place. They also are assumed to be non-reoccurring events.

While justification is thought to be the result of *initial* faith, sanctification is viewed as the result of *continuing* faith. If man continues in his faith, all parts of Christendom agree that he will

---

[1] The forgiveness is specified as the removal of the *eternal penalty* resting upon his sins. This, its proponent thinks, keeps this view from the difficulties arising from the need of additional forgiveness in the Scriptures (cf., Matt. 6:14-15; 18:21-25; 1John 1:9; etc.). This is cleaver, but is it really presented this way in Scripture?

[2] In some Christian traditions this is not a permanent standing that necessarily lasts forever. It can be lost, and the person can need to regain it again. But if the Christian's walk is what it should be, it will be everlasting, all agree.

[3] Again, some think this is initially true, but can be lost and can need to be regained.

[4] But the reader should be aware that a new explanation of justification is being taught today. In it justification is broken down into an *initial* justification and then a *final* justification. This development, in my opinion, is an attempt to make room for good works in justification. It is generally believed that justification is essentially separate from good works while, at the same time, it supposedly results in good works necessarily and inevitably. As long as the historical theology of the Reformation continues to be clung to, justification will remain in a confused state.

be finally delivered into the present of God in heaven. But many believe that if man does not continue in his faith, then he ultimately ends up in hell. While there are quite different explanations about the process that produces eternal condemnation, it is agreed that a person's spiritual walk with God, subsumed under the rubric of sanctification in the graph, actually indicates to a great extent a person's eternal destiny. *Such a walk must be present for heaven to be gained.* Without that walk not only is heaven

Justification	Sanctification	Glorification
X_(_____X_____)_X		
• Initial Faith	• Continuing Faith	• The End of Faith
• Birth	• Growth	• Translation into
• Redemption	• Walk with God	Heaven
• Reconciliation		
• Ransom, Propitiation, Salvation		

unreachable, but hell becomes the only option for that person.

And glorification is supposed to be the ultimate transformation that takes place, generally speaking, the moment a person arrives in heaven. He will be *in glory* and will *be glorified* just like the body of his Lord. All physical weaknesses and inabilities are removed as the believer puts on immortality.[1] Being *in glory, then,* is another way of saying a person is *in heaven.* But as we will discover, the term glory has too many different referents for it to be limited and reduced to just one idea.

Heaven will be a time when earthly faith is no more. At that time each person will live in a dynamic, loving relationship with God after his Biblical hope has become his present reality. It is for this reason that Paul stated in 1Cor. 13:13 that of faith, hope,

---

[1] 1Cor. 15:53-54.

and love, the greatest of these three is love because only it continues on into eternity.

All of this should sound quite familiar. Now comes the hard part. As we examine the Scriptures and allow them to revise the construct of the paradigm that best reflects the true message of the Bible, we must be willing to change our perspectives to whatever the Scriptures set before us as facts. Its statements, and not man's syntheses, must form the grid of our understanding of life. What follows now are some of those facts of Scripture that force us to change our diagram.

Unlike the previous diagram, this one starts off suggesting that *justification, as the other paradigm understood it, does not exist.* The other paradigm told us that justification, whatever it is, took place at initial faith. But since there is not one example of initial faith in any of the thirty-nine books of the OT, it ought to be plain that no one is able to tell anyone else what happens at initial faith. If initial faith is never mentioned, described, or discussed in the Scriptures, no one can speak authoritatively about it. And that is the first fact of Scripture!

Justification, as Reformed theology developed it in the sixteenth and seventeenth centuries, became the foundation upon which all of the aspects of salvation rested. Obviously, if it there is a problem with justification, then everything that is based upon it will be in jeopardy as well. There is a justification in the Bible, but it turns out to be very different from the one that the Reformers created to fulfill the needs of their theology. What if the early church had it right after all? What if justification really is a subset of sanctification? If a person will simply try to think that through, he will immediately become aware of the huge difference such a shift makes relative to man's spiritual condition.

Sanctification[1]			
Ø_____X_____X_____X_____X			

- Initial Faith Not
  Mentioned
        - Continuing Faith
        - Growth
        - Walk with God
        - Justification (J+)
        (Do redemption, reconciliation, ransom, and
        propitiation go here too? It seems so.)

Since the OT never mentions initial faith, it is strongly urged that it shouldn't be expected to be present in the NT either. Consequently, what has become possibly *the focal point* of Christian theology is never mentioned in the Scriptures, or at least never emphasized in the Scriptures. Such a fact ought to put us all on guard. Maybe we've been led down the wrong path entirely. When we make our focus what the Scriptures never mention, we have built our theology without a foundation, standing only on the piers and beams in our own minds. Only our own pride will keep us from being troubled about this fact.[2]

> Everywhere in the NT it is clear that those who began to believe in Jesus had already believed in the God who had sent Him into the world.

It is true that we find lots of people coming to initial faith in Jesus in the NT. But that is what one ought to expect. It is impossible to believe a truth or believe in a person until it or He

---

[1] Abbreviations will be used because of a lack of space. S+ refers to sanctification; Sv refers to Salvation; G+ refers to glorification; and J+ refers to justification.

[2] Cf., e.g., Prov. 16:5, 6, 18.

has been revealed. So, no one could believe in Jesus before He came upon the human scene. Believing in a coming Messiah is not the same thing as believing in Jesus. The Gospels of the NT teach us this plainly. If it were the same, then all those who believed in a coming Messiah would have believed in Jesus as the Messiah. But not all did. And it is a great mistake to *assume* that initial faith in Jesus is necessarily a person's initial faith in God.

Not one example of initial faith is as clear-cut as it is universally assumed to be. Nowhere in the four Gospels is there an example of someone who believes in Jesus but who had not already believed in God the Father. And with the importance that our traditional theology places on the concept of a *presumed* initial faith, one would expect to find examples of it everywhere. But that is not so!

Only in the book of Acts are there examples of individuals who trusted in Jesus that *may not* have had some previous faith in God. But these are highly uncertain and inadequate to base any inherently convincing argument upon. When the Scriptures' testimony of God's communication to all men is received,[1] one becomes predisposed to reject even the possibility that there might be someone who does not know God even when he is obviously not following Him as he should. God's revelation is both clear and sufficient, leaving man without excuse. While this revelation can, of course, be suppressed as Paul tells us in Rom. 1:18-20, the act of suppressing it establishes the fact that God has made Himself clearly known even to such a person.

---

[1] I dealt with this aspect of God's revelation and its effectiveness in my book, *The Prodigal Paradigm*. The Scriptures are clearer on this issue than many may want to admit. Cf., Gen. 9:17; Ps. 19:1-6; 24:1 (2-6); 82:8; 100:1-3; John 1:9; Rom. 1:18-20; Acts 14:14-17; 17:26-27; etc.

Sanctification			
Ø_____X_____X_____X_____X_			

—.

- Initial Faith Not
  Mentioned
    - Continuing Faith
    - Growth
    - Walk with God
    - Justification (J+)
    (Do redemption, reconciliation, ransom, and propitiation go here too?)

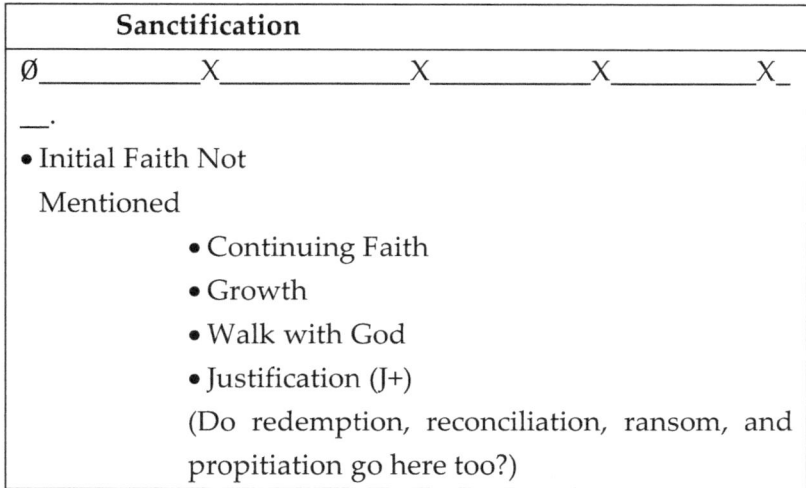

Since there is no emphasis upon anyone's initial faith in the Scriptures, we must begin the construction of our paradigm with that fact. Without going into detail, everything that has been believed to be involved at initial faith must be moved to another place in the diagram because there is no initial faith to be found in the Bible.

And with that move enormous ramifications arise. So, for example, forgiveness of sins and a declared right standing with God was thought to be needed and given at initial faith. But if there is no point of initial faith, then either these things aren't needed as was first supposed, or they must be inserted at other points along the graph. And with their change in position a change in their meaning and significance is necessarily required.

Notice in the new graph that justification has been moved to a spot below sanctification. Justification has been historically identified more with a person's *birth* than with his *growth*, and more with his *standing* before God than with his *walk* with God. Essentially, justification has been seen as God's gracious declaration of a man's acceptance into the family of God forevermore. He is forgiven of all the sins he has committed or ever will commit. And most importantly, he is given a righteousness that becomes an effective shield against all accusations that could ever be laid at his doorstep to disqualify him from attaining his heavenly destiny.

But since there is no initial faith found in the Scriptures, it should be quite obvious that man's synthesis of the Scriptural teaching on justification is incorrect. *Justification, rather than being a one-time event, is God's repeated declaration over a person's walk, affirming its righteous character.* And if the present verdict is not justification, then it must be condemnation, signifying that God's righteous standard was not achieved presently.

Probably one of the easiest and most assured corrections to make in our contemporary theology is to *reject the idea that justification happens only once and to accept the fact that it is actually a repeated phenomenon.* So, for example, Abraham is said to have been justified twice, once when he believed the promise of God for a multitudinous progeny[1] and again when he offered up Isaac on an altar.[2] These two justifications were separated by at least fifteen years and possibly as many as twenty-five years. Consequently, they cannot be describing the same event.

Another correction to the doctrine of justification that is easy to make springs from the observation that *in neither instance of Abraham's two justifications was he forgiven of his past sins nor imputed with (or given) a righteousness that was not rightfully his* (according to God's own accounting or crediting) *by responding in faith to God's promise to him or to God's requirement of him.* Abra-

---

[1] Gen. 15:6; Rom. 4:1-3, 22-25.
[2] Js. 2:21-24.

ham's first justification did not require works; his second one did. Forgiveness and receiving a gift from Christ of His righteousness simply aren't involved in justification as we have been led to believe.

In neither of Abraham's justifications was initial faith being exercised. In like fashion, Rahab was justified possibly as many as forty years after her faith in the God of Israel had begun to change her life. But regardless of how long it was between her realization that Israel's God was the true God of heaven and earth and her justification by Him recorded in the epistle of James, two truths are incontrovertible: 1.) the justification that James refers to did not occur at her realization that Israel's God was the true God, and 2.) her justification involved works. James *explicitly* told his readers that Rahab "was justified by works."

Consequently, if we ask, "When was it that she was justified?" The Scriptural testimony answers that question and says that her justification occurred "when she received the messengers and sent them out by another way!"[1] It is quite clear that Rahab had believed in the God of Israel for some time before He justified her act of faith that James mentioned.[2]

Every time we see a *personal* example of justification in the Scriptures, it describes how God views the response that a trusting person is giving. God justified King David's response which was certainly not his initial faith in Him.[3] The publican's response was justified or commended by God while the Pharisee's response was not.[4] The Jewish leaders, who already believed in Yahweh and in His promised Messiah, standing before Jesus

---

[1] Js. 2:25.

[2] Js. 2:25; Josh. 2:8-15.

[3] Rom. 4:6-8.

[4] Lk. 18:9-14.

would receive God's justification *if* they gave the right answer to Jesus' claims about being their Messiah.[1] The term is used quite consistently, always denoting God's evaluation of a response given by someone who was trying to walk with Him.

Consequently, we are forced to place justification under sanctification, as the early church had done, because it is obviously another element or perspective on sanctification. While sanctification properly describes the Holy Spirit's transformation of a person's character as he walks with God,[2] justification is God's analysis of that walk.[3] Every response that God says meets His standard He justifies. Every choice that doesn't meet His standard He condemns. When He justifies a response, He declares that it was righteous because it was done in faith.[4] When he condemns a response, He declares that it was unrighteous, regardless of how moral it might have been, or how much in conformity to the

> Justification is a declaration *over the present moment of a person's life*, not over his past history, nor, much less, over his future.

standard of obedience expected from him, because it was not performed in faith.[5]

But the point that I've tried to make over and over is that justification is a declaration of *what is already present or what is already true* of a person or in his response. In justification God is declaring that the man is doing the right thing and he is doing it in the right way, the required way, namely, in faith.

---

[1] Matt. 12:22-37.

[2] E.g., 2Cor. 3:17-18; Rom. 8:28-29; Gal. 4:19.

[3] E.g., Lk. 18:14.

[4] E.g., Gen. 15:6; Rom. 4:3, 22-25.

[5] E.g., Rom. 10:2-3.

S+	Salvation
Ø_____X_____X_____X_____X	

- Initial Faith
  No Mention

  - Walk with God
  - Justification (J+)
  - Ransom
  - Redemption
  - Reconciliation
  Propitiation

- Continuing Faith
  (now in Jesus too)
- Regeneration (the
  new birth)
- Eternal life and the
  Holy Spirit

We can clarify the issue by asking a couple of questions. When you respond to God's leading, are you doing what God has directed you to do and are you doing it as you trust God to intervene in your circumstances? If your response did find approval with God, and it will every time that it is done in faith, then He declared it righteous and not subject to a reevaluation by any other person at any later date.

As we look back at the diagram, we must realize that the concepts of ransom, redemption, and propitiation, all of which have been presumed to occur at the same moment as justification, have no theologically acceptable slot on the diagram once justification is moved. I can show the importance of this move by asking a couple of questions: "If Jesus' payment on the cross for man's sins does not belong at the beginning of the diagram, then where does it belong, and what function does it perform at the place that it is inserted?"

Our traditional theological construct or formulation has no place else for it to fit other than at the very beginning. It must fit there because it is necessary for our initial, eternal acceptance with God, we are told. Without a belief in Jesus' payment for a person's sins, no one can move from the *unbeliever* status to the *believer* status. No one can move from being *eternally condemned* to being *eternally saved*. At least that is the teaching that we've been given, right?

But the truth is those are *assumptions*, one and all. We must go back to the Scriptures to test the connections between these various, theological ideas. Are these connections valid? Or are they unfounded associations which many have *presumed* to be true without any Biblical facts to support them?

We are forced by the testimony of the Scriptures to place justification under the concept of sanctification. We understand that placing justification there signifies that it describes a person's *continuing* faith rather than his supposed *initial* faith.

Hence, justification can't be a once-for-all matter.

We must also realize that since it relates to a person's continuing faith, it must rarely be connected the issue of any forgiveness of sins. Because it involves the continuing faith of an individual, it is a positive declaration about the righteousness that God is crediting to his continuing faith.

Furthermore, since justification is about his continuing faith, the righteousness that God declares upon this person is a continuing accumulation of righteous deeds, rather than a once for all gift of righteousness to a person.

We also realize that the death of Christ Jesus relates to a person's *walk* with God and not to his *supposed* initial (and *supposed* further, eternal) acceptance by God. And *that*, if you haven't grasped it yet, is a very big deal! In fact, it may be at the epicenter of the theological tremors you are beginning to feel. But their ramifications stagger a person's imagination.

S+	Salvation

Ø_____X_____X_____X_____X_

__.

- Initial Faith
  No Mention

  - Continuing
    Faith
  - Growth
  - Walk with God
  - Justification (J+)
  - Ransom
  - Redemption
  - Reconciliation
    Propitiation

- Continuing Faith
  (now in Jesus too)
  - Regeneration (the
    new birth)
  - Eternal life and the
    Holy Spirit

As you look back at the diagram, you will notice that not a word has been said about any *spiritual salvation* to this point. That means that spiritual salvation is not related to *a supposed initial* faith, or to either justification or sanctification *per se*. The Scriptures know nothing of any spiritual salvation until Jesus began His earthly ministry. *That means that people in the OT could have been justified and sanctified without ever being saved.* Consequently, if it was not offered in the OT, it must not be read back into any text of the OT. Spiritual salvation is uniquely a NT phenomenon begun by Jesus during His earthly ministry.

When we find Jesus offering to *save* those who trust in Him, we encounter something entirely new in the Bible. And it is very important to observe that He was offering this salvation to people[1] who already were pursuing God in faith. In other words, Jesus was offering to save people who were already, to varying degrees, pleasing to God. In fact, God was already approving of their spiritual walk, and yet He offered them a salvation that would be a wonderful experience in their walk.

Those who believed in and walked with God in the OT were translated into heaven to be with God after their physical deaths. Representative of this group of people are Moses,[2] Abraham, Isaac, and Jacob. Jesus clearly affirmed this truth about them in His discussion with the Sadducees on the resurrection.[3]

> *Salvation* is never connected to one's eternal destiny.

But this happened to them all *without their being saved* in the contemporary sense of that term. *There simply was no transaction in the OT that the Bible describes as spiritual salvation and yet heaven was still gained.*

If heaven can be gained without salvation in the OT, that suggests that salvation is not about going to heaven. Rather, it is wholly an *earthly matter*. It can be either physical or spiritual in nature. But it is always related to matters or circumstances taking place on earth. It does not gain a person an afterlife.

As I have explained earlier, salvation has at least five different aspects to it. It is up to the student to *rightly divide*[4] the possibilities as each context de-

> Context is king; theology is his temptress.

mands. But for our purposes it is important to observe that a

---

[1] I would use the terms "believer" here except for the fact that the term *believer* has been infused with so many unbiblical ideas that to use it can create more confusion.

[2] At the transfiguration Moses appeared with Jesus alongside of Elijah who had been translated alive into heaven (2Kgs. 2:1, 11).

[3] Cf., Matt. 22:23-33.

[4] Cf., 2Tim. 2:15.

right belief in God and even a *consistent* walk with God can be seen in the Bible in *both* Testaments without *salvation* being true of that person. All salvations today prepare a person for the salvation that delivers one into the age of Messiah's kingdom.

The life that Jesus gives at the moment of belief in Him is termed *eternal life* in the Bible. The depth of confusion that exists among Christians is crystalized in the fact that *eternal life has little to do with eternity*. It is, rather, all about the life that can be lived in time, in this earthly sphere, throughout one's earthly existence. As a result one can rightly affirm that the focus of the NT boils down to the following two points: 1.) obtaining through faith in Jesus the new life that He offers, and 2.) learning how to access the life that Jesus has given and walk by it so that one can experience the spiritual victory over the trials and difficulties that God has deemed it wise for him to face. Many have discovered this life. Seek them out to explain it to you.

The next element in the diagram is glorification. This word is entirely a theological term. While various terms for glory and glorify can be found in the Scriptures, the concept of people *longing to go to glory* is not an emphasis of the Scriptures. Neither is the idea emphasized that when a person finally arrives in heaven, he is then *glorified*. For sure, there is some truth to these ideas. But they are hardly foci of the Scriptures. The Bible is about *living a life of fellowship with God while upon the earth, and representing Him in all that we do now*.

> The story of Job describes the invisible conflict behind the scenes of life until the Messianic Age begins.

Because that is the focus of the Scriptures, it should come as no surprise that the term *glorification* is related to life upon this earth more than anything else. In

145

fact, it best describes Jesus' coming kingdom upon the earth when all things are renewed, and the curse is removed from it.[1] The glory of His reign over a renewed earth will be beyond any experience anyone has had throughout earthly history.

After glorification, which on the diagram is described as "serving in the Messianic Age," then comes eternity. The Messianic Age is the millennial reign of Jesus Christ upon this earth during which He fulfills all the covenants and promises given to Israel in the OT. After that one thousand year reign comes eternity.

The topic of eternity does not fall within the scope of our present study or focus. There are several different ideas about eternity that need to be taken more seriously than we normally take them. It is included here only for the sake of establishing the fact that God has a plan that will continue beyond the present life on earth. At that time God will execute His desired will in every part of the new system perfectly. There will be no evil or sin. Over all once again He will proclaim, "It is very good!"

The message of the Bible may be likened to the story of Job, described in chapters one and two, lived out over and over throughout human history. Man is caught in the middle of a spiritual warfare between God and Satan. On the one hand, God has revealed Himself to and blessed man in various ways. And man has responded to these overtures in varying degrees of obedience, some more and some less. Satan is using all the means that God will permit him to employ to lead man far away from Him. Both man and Satan will be held accountable for living independently of God and His will.

---

[1] Cf., e.g., Rom. 8:17-25.

To summarize the diagram, then, it can be said that *Saul demonstrates wonderfully well the distinction between a **justified** person and a person seeking to obtain the great prize of a future, earthly salvation (i.e., the deliverance into Messiah's kingdom upon this earth)*. He had walked with the one, true God **before** he ever trusted in Jesus. But when he trusted in Jesus, he received eternal life, that is, the new life that wonderfully transforms as it enables a person to live righteously. Saul would gladly give up all that he had accomplished in his previous walk with God for the privilege of being found in Christ having a righteousness that was not his own but was a result of the life of Jesus flowing through him by faith.

Jesus has come to offer both forgiveness for those who have not been walking closely with God and a supernatural life to enable each person to overcome all the trials and afflictions that are being faced in this world. That life will enable each person to have a taste of what life will be like in the glorious age of the coming kingdom, communing with the God of the universe as he represents Him in all that he does. So, when Jesus said,

"I have come that you might have life and have it abundantly,"[1]

He was offering exactly what each person needs to overcome the spiritual warfare that leaves brokenness, isolationism, and purposelessness in its wake.

---

[1] John 10:10b.

EPILOGUE

As you are well aware, both of the books in this series have left several questions that need to be addressed yet untouched. This is actually by design. When you teach something completely new, there is only so much that a person can absorb at one time. I intend to add layer after layer of explanation in the books that follow. But for the sake of simplicity, I am trying to limit each discussion to the main issues and not address all the ramifications that naturally follow from them.

It is quite obvious that several issues need to be addressed such as the whole idea of "salvation," the death of Christ, and the non-salvific reasons for Christ's appearing. I have planned a book on each topic to round out this series. And if this series succeeds in creating a thirst for walking with God, as I hope it does, the next series will be devoted to explaining that most important topic of all: How do we walk in intimate fellowship with the God of all creation? May God put that desire upon all of our hearts more passionately than ever before.

www.ingramcontent.com/pod-product-compliance
Lightning Source LLC
LaVergne TN
LVHW051240080426
835513LV00016B/1684